The Sol Plaatje European Union
Poetry Anthology

Vol X

# The Sol Plaatje European Union Poetry Anthology

Volume X

Selected by Mongane Wally Serote,
Goodenough Mashego, Pieter Odendaal,
Innocentia Mhlambi, Neo Sehlahla
& Rustum Kozain

The views and opinions expressed in this publication are not necessarily those of the funder.

First published by Jacana Media (Pty) Ltd in 2021

10 Orange Street
Sunnyside
Auckland Park 2092
South Africa
+2711 628 3200
www.jacana.co.za

© Individual contributers, 2021
All rights reserved.

Cover photograph © Alexia Webster (www.alexiawebster.com)
Front cover image: A man helps one of the younger Kaapse Klopse get ready for the Cape Town Tweede Nuwe Jaar carnival celebrations in Bo Kaap, Cape Town, 17 January 2015.

ISBN 978-1-4314-3132-8

Set in Ehrhardt 11/13pt
Printed and bound by XMD Books, Cape Town
Job no. 003804

See a complete list of Jacana titles at www.jacana.co.za

CONTENTS

Message from the Sponsor *EU Ambassador to South Africa, Dr Riina Kionka* xi

Foreword, *Dr Mongane Wally Serote* xiii

IPENI LISA PHAKAMA, *Thansanqa Mlungisi Cindi* 1
THE PEN STILL RISES, an English translation by *Innocentia Mhlambi* 2
TO SAVE A COUNTRY, *Connor Shay Cogill* 3
STONES AND FEATHERS, *Christine Coates* 5
MAMMIE, *Florence Diana de Vries* 6
MOMMY, an English translation by *Pieter Odendaal* 8
BROOD EN TEE, *Kimberly Elana Fray* 10
BREAD AND TEA, an English translation by *Pieter Odendaal* .. 12
MOSADI GARE GA BASADI, *Kgalalelo Lebogang Gaebee* 14
WOMAN OF VIRTUE, an English translation by *Goodenough Mashego* 15
NAKO E FITLHILE, *Kgalalelo Lebogang Gaebee*............ 16
IT'S TIME, an English translation by *Goodenough Mashego*..... 18
II-V-I, *Mamodiehi Gwala* 20
NOT YET UHURU, *Bhekumuzi Christopher Kubheka* 21
BOTHATA BA HAO KENG?, *Thabiso Tsietsi Lakajoe*........ 22
WHAT IS YOUR PROBLEM?, an English translation by *Goodenough Mashego* 24
MOHANUA, *Thabiso Tsietsi Lakajoe*...................... 26
THE REJECTED ONE, an English translation by *Goodenough Mashego* 27
ZWA MISHUMONI, *Tshindane Livhuwani* 28
THE WORKPLACE, an English translation by *Neo Sehlanhla* .. 29

TRIMETHYLAMINE, *Alinaswe Lusengo* 30
THE MEMORIES OF VIOLENCE, *Zama Madinana* 32
NOTES FROM RATANANG TAVERN, *Zama Madinana* 33
IMFAZWE YEZIYOBISI, *Landisile Magwaxaza* 35
WAR ON DRUGS, *an English translation by Innocentia Mhlambi* 37
LEBOKO, *James Mahlangu* 39
POEM, *an English translation by Goodenough Mashego* 40
LORATO, *James Mahlangu* 41
LOVE, *an English translation by Goodenough Mashjudeego* 42
WEDDINGS AND FUNERALS, *Nolwazi Mbali Mahlangu* .. 43
GE NKABE O LE GONA, *Tshepiso Makgoloane* 45
IF YOU WERE HERE, *an English translation by Goodenough Mashego* 47
DIKATA, *Charles Julie Makofane* 49
DIKATA, *an English translation by Goodenough Mashego* 50
RE HLOBOGA PIDIBIDI, *Tebogo Patricia Mamabolo* 51
WE MOURN DUCKLING, *an English translation by Goodenough Mashego* 53
MHLABA, MY SON, *Maakomele R. Manaka* 55
THE LAST STRETCH, *Adré Marshall* 58
HOME LIKE A TOMB, *Keketso Adorn Mashigo* 59
MADODA KWANELE, *Zongezile Matshoba* 61
MEN IT IS ENOUGH, *an English translation by Innocentia Mhlambi* 62
KHUTHAZEKA KE BHINQ' ELIHLE, *Mzoli Mavimbela* ... 63
BE MOTIVATED BEAUTIFUL WOMAN, *an English translation by Innocentia Mhlambi* 65
GRANNY, *Frank Meintjies* 67
BAYAPHI UBUNTU, *Mandlakayise Mfanta* 68

WHERE HAS HUMANITY GONE, *an English translation by Innocentia Mhlambi* 70

O FIHLILE, *Mmabore Gladys Mogashoa* 72

YOU ARRIVED, *an English translation by Goodenough Mashego* 75

FOR MY UNCLES (MANDLA AND JABU) IN EXILE, *Siza Nkosi-Mokhele* 78

LEFU LA MORENA HINTSHA KA 1835, *Tsela Jeffrey Moloi* 81

THE DEATH OF HINTSA IN 1835, *an English translation by Goodenough Mashego* 82

NTATE SOBUKWE, *Tsela Jeffrey Moloi* 83

FATHER SOBUKWE, *an English translation by Goodenough Mashego* 86

SS MENDI, *Tsela Jeffrey Moloi*........................... 89

SS MENDI, *an English translation by Goodenough Mashego* 92

GENETIC LOTTERY, *Nedine Moonsamy* 95

E HLAGILE, *Mapule Ramaila Moswane* 96

IT HAS HAPPENED, *an English translation by Goodenough Mashego* 98

BHAQ' OLUNGAMUNWE, *Aphiwe Masibonge Namba* 100

LIGHT THAT CANNOT BE COMPARED, *an English translation by Innocentia Mhlambi* 101

CAMAGU, *Kwazi Ndlangisa* 102

CAMAGU, *and English translation by Innocentia Mhlambi*..... 103

IZOLO-KUSASA, *Kwazi Ndlangisa*...................... 104

YESTERDAY-TOMORROW, *an English translation by Innocentia Mhlambi* 106

EKHAYA KUTHULE, *Mawushe Selby Nomnganga* 108

IT IS QUIET AT HOME, *an English translation by Innocentia Mhlambi*.. 109

ZAPHEL' IIMBOKODO, *Azile Ntloni* 110
WOMEN ARE BEING FINISHED, *an English translation by Innocentia Mhlambi* 112
KWANELE, *Sihle Ntuli* 114
IT IS ENOUGH, *an English translation by Innocentia Mhlambi* 116
MONNA KE NKU, *Mosima Kagiso Phakane* 118
MEN DON'T CRY, *an English translation by Goodenough Mashego* 120
SELLO SA MOSADI, *Mosima Kagiso Phakane* 122
THE CRY OF A WOMAN, *an English translation by Goodenough Mashego* 124
ISIKHALO SOMFAZI OMNYAMA!, *Yvonne Busisiwe Phyllis*... 126
A BLACK WOMAN'S CRY!, *an English translation by Innocentia Mhlambi* 127
I AM YOUR DAUGHTER, *Tshifhiwa Itai Ratshiungo* 128
THE NATIVE CHOICE, *Warren Jeremy Rourke* 131
MY MOTHER'S HOUSE, *Dimakatso Anthea Sedite* 132
ON THE PEOPLE'S POWER, *Noluthando Mpho Sibisi*...... 133
MALOHLE, *Moses Seletiša* 134
MALOHLE, *an English translation by Goodenough Mashego* ... 135
UMZILI ONGAPHEZI, *Siwaphiwe Fortune Shweni*......... 136
A MOURNER WHO DOES NOT STOP, *an English translation by Innocentia Mhlambi* 138
ISIKHALO SAMANINA, *Yonela Thengimfene*............. 140
THE CRY OF WOMEN, *an English translation by Innocentia Mhlambi*... 141
IZIHANGE, *Anelisa Thengimfene*....................... 142
SAVAGES, *an English translation by Innocentia Mhlambi*...... 144
NTWA YA BANA BA THARI, *Thabang Tsolo* 146

CIVIL WAR, *an English translation by Goodenough Mashego* ... 147
SELLO SA MMOKOTSANE, *Thabang Tsolo* 148
A WEEPING, *an English translation by Goodenough Mashego* .. 150
BIRDSONG OF THE EASTERN CAPE, *David Jude van Schoor* 152
MATCHBOX, *Justin Lyndon Williams*. 155
THESE DAYS, *Lucas Delisiwe Zulu*..................... 156

Biographies 157
What is the European Union?.......................... 173

A MESSAGE FROM DR RIINA KIONKA, EUROPEAN UNION AMBASSADOR TO SOUTH AFRICA

Poetry permits the expression of emotion within defined parameters. And for that reason, it heightens those emotions themselves. Like squeezing a tube of toothpaste whose cap is only a little bit open.

This is why I love poetry (and sometimes give in to temptation to pen some, myself). By disciplining oneself with form and rhythm, it's possible to give the spirit freer rein.

Personal sentiments, I admit. But they trigger a much deeper question: how relevant is poetry in our modern and increasingly fractured world?

It is probably safe to say that the world in which we live has in the past decade become a lot less predictable for a majority of people everywhere. The only constant seems to be change and that seems to be accelerating all the time.

The old way of doing things, of communicating, of meeting and sharing experiences and thoughts are increasingly challenged everywhere. Technology has been at the centre of this profound impact on human interactions and relations. The Covid-19 pandemic we are some distance from putting behind us has been ... and will continue to be ... an unprecedented accelerator.

There is a paradox: while technology has on so many levels brought us closer together and in effect has made our world so much smaller, it simultaneously has also alienated us on an interpersonal level.

Poetry bridges the gap. In its immediacy, poetry acts as a conduit that helps us overcome that lack of personal contact … it helps us share the unsaid and captures and communicates not only thoughts, but more importantly emotions, feelings and impressions.

The very fact that the Sol Plaatje European Union Poetry Award and anthology turn ten with this edition, that the anthology continues to sell well, and that the award continues to attract a wide range of submissions in South Africa's many official languages, is clear evidence that poetry remains as relevant as ever.

Thank you to all the poets who submitted their work/s and congratulations to this edition's three winners. The Sol Plaatje European Union Poetry Award has provided a platform for you to have forever woven into the country's consciousness, into its literary fabric, your perceptions, thoughts and sentiments.

A very special acknowledgement to the eminent panel of judges, and at its head, South Africa's deeply respected Poet Laureate, Professor Mongane Wally Serote. Your dedication to this project has shaped a lasting legacy. Thank you for your commitment and support.

And finally, a word of thanks to our partners and the driving force behind this wonderful initiative, Jacana Media and the non-profit Jacana Literary Foundation. May this initiative continue to prosper in good times and in the not-so-good. Thank you for having made this project a reality for the past decade.

FOREWORD

Among the many gifts our country gave to Sol Plaatje is that he was multilingual. As the language issue looms large in our country – in a negative way – it is asking us once more whether we know that we are a multilingual country, and if so, what are we doing about it?

Do we remember that this issue of multilingualism is a rare national treasure? The matter of African languages must be raised in this manner during the tenth anniversary of the Sol Plaatje European Union Poetry Anthology because, as an anthology which promotes multilingualism through poetry, it has achieved the status of being one of the important multilingual poetry platforms in the country.

It must be of great national concern that even twenty-five years after our constitution declared that 'The official languages of the Republic are Sepedi, Sesotho, Setswana, siSwati, Tshivenda, Xitsonga, Afrikaans, English, isiNdebele and isiZulu…', African languages are still marginalised. They are marginalised because there is an unwritten implication that if one is not an English speaker, one will not be functional in the nation except as a labourer or, worst still, that the person is not civilised.

It is generally unofficially suggested by white culture that one of the reasons why black pupils flock to former Model C schools is because they will be taught in English, not only to be civilised, but also so that they become intelligent and therefore functional within the capitalist economy. There is nothing wrong in being taught in English if your mother tongue is different, but there is everything wrong if you are taught English only at the expense of your mother tongue. The risk is that one can be a professional student for life because one has to learn white culture and therefore also learn the English language forever and unlearn it forever within one's own mother tongue context!

I raise this issue against the backdrop of literature in our country. At that, while I must admit that there has been committed and focused attempts at ensuring professional translations of poetry in the Sol Plaatje European Union Poetry Anthology, much more professionalism is needed. Also, the issue here must not be to shoot the messenger, but to raise matters at the level of institutions guided by the constitution to answer the question: has the nation done everything possible to ensure that African languages are empowered through their being adequately resourced, both materially and through professional personnel and institutions, and to ensure that they are promoted within their historical and cultural context?

While the fact must not be lost that the constitution states in part that:

'A Pan South African Language Board established by national legislation must-:
- (a) promote and create conditions for the development and use of
- all official languages,
- the Khoi, Nama and San languages…'

It must be noted that, historically, colonialism and the apartheid system had by law marginalised African culture

– and therefore languages also – precisely because Africans were seen as machines to be systematically exploited and utilised to eke, in every way possible, all the wealth of the country for the benefit of Europeans who were considered more civilised.

It is long overdue that a collective consisting of the public sector, private sector and the organs of civil society, having been empowered by legislation, create training centres for translations and interpretation facilities and language laboratories. Beginning at the Sol Plaatje University in Kimberly and at other institutions of higher learning also as a reference base for the Pan South African Language Board (Pansalb), it is certain that we would collectively, as a nation, hear things we have not heard before; the cultural expressions and wisdoms, which are inherent and intrinsic to the collective cultural expressions and wisdoms in our languages – especially African languages.

More important is that it would be one of the most valuable contributions to the cohesion of the nation. It is most appropriate to raise this issue in the context of a project named after Sol Plaatje, one of the outstanding multilinguists of our country!

I have raised this matter in this way precisely because the Sol Plaatje European Union Poetry Anthology has, as a platform of multilingual poetry expression, attracted poets from across the language spectrum of our country. I note this as such because the poets, not being objects of history, are in search for how to become masters of history. Their poetic context and language expression note that language has never ever not been an issue of conflict and strife in our country.

NOTES FROM RATANANG TAVERN
Zama Madinana

they
come here
with scabs
they cannot sing

to wash
their rusted past
in the waters of babylon

they come here
to close
their spiritual abyss

the sick
the poor
& the broken

they soak
tavern walls
in swamps of semen

floods of urine
taunt no man
here

yelling armpits
halt
no tot
of vodka

clouds of ganja smoke
cloak & choke
no laughter
here

here we dodge
flying bricks
& beer bottles
even
the blobs of vomit
cannot tame
the drunken feet
from dancing
to the maskanda rhythms

but songs
of hope-erosion
continue to rape black dignity

how do you escape
a carnage of dreams
in a community of nervous ambitions

CAMAGU
Kwazi Ndlangisa
(Zulu)

Ngiwukukhanya ezweni labansundu,
Ngixosha ubumnyama bungekazalwa kuhle bonyenzi
ebusweni bomhlaba/
Ngingowenzalo ezweni laseAfrika
Ufakazi, bheka ubudlelwano besikhumba sami nelanga
Ngazalwa ngowesifazane njengakho konke okuhamba

phezu kwalomhlaba
Amandla ngawembeswa ngookhokho nookhokhokazi
endulo mina ngingekazalwa nangomcabango
Ngimdala kunami
Ngimncane ezweni
Kwamoya kukhulwa ezweni lamathongo,
Ungibona nje angibazi ubuthongo bakwaMhlaba
Ngithwele izintaba namagquma ezizukulwana zakwaNtu,
amaphupho nezifiso ezafel' emafini zicinga ukukhanya
kwelanga
Zazihamba nokukhanya zingazelele
Lokhu kuyangibulala
Hleze futhi khona lokhu kuyangiphilisa
Pho ke mina bengiyini ngingabanga wuhlanya,
Nakhu ngibhadula lapho livuka nanxa lidonsa izikhumba
ilanga
Yimi lowo ngilandela amaloba wezithunywa zikaMenzi
ehlane nasemkhathini
Inhloso ukuthola izimpendulo zayizolo ukuze
ngikhanyisele inamuhla
Ngesiqubulo sika Makukhanye, sithokoze isizwe
sakwaMoya.
Camagu!

CAMAGU
Kwazi Ndlangia

I am the light in the land of brown people,
I chase away darkness before it is birthed just like the
morning star on the face of the earth
I am a descendant of Afrika
Evidence, look at the relationship of my skin and the sun
I was born of a woman just like everything on the face of

the earth
My powers were given to me by my ancestors long ago before I was conceived as thought
I am older than myself
I am the youngest in the world
Just like wind one grows up in the world of the ancestors
As you see me I do not know the sleep of the Earth
I am carrying mountains and hills of the generations of Humanity,
Dreams and aspirations that died in the clouds looking for light
They travelled with light unawares
That this is killing me
Perhaps this too also gives me life
So how can it be that I am not mad,
Here I am walking aimlessly when the sun rises and sets
Here I am following the writings of the messengers of the Creator in the fields and forests
The aim is to get answers of yesterday so that I shine the light for today
All hailing Makukhanye, the nation of Moya is pleased. Camagu!

(an English translation by Innocentia Mhlambi)

O FIHLILE
Mmabore Gladys Mogashoa
Sepedi

O fihlile bana ba Thulare re sa ipikitla malaka
Mabarebare re a kwele ka wene
Gore phokgo o sa le ka mošola
O fihla le go tšhuba hlaga

O paletšwe le go tamiša ka mafateng a matelele
O reng wa hloka molao
Bja gago bohodu bo kgotsiša le mmopi
A gona o morwa mang?

O tumutše mekgapa ka medu
A gao swiela a matala digatlela ro ithekga kae?
O pharola metshere
Bana re a golola
O laola lefase ka bophara o le tee
O nabile le ge ka a nama re sa go bone
Re kopane natšo ra di kgona
Phokgo o fegediša le boramahlale

O tsošitše dipolelo
O re swarišitše sekatapowana
Tša mararankodi a sebjalebjale ditaba di re kgebiša segošane
Re sepipamoyeng ga re sa kgona

Tšatši ka tšatši go go iwa mabitleng
A ya gago mpa ga e tlale?
O phura mamane le bommabo
O swana le tsheola thaba Leolo
Ditšhiwana ga re tsebe o wela kae
O iphetošitše tlou o re gata boka magokolodi
O gaketše bo ka mokopa wa thaba

O tswalela difero ka magora
O tswalela mešomo motswalago tlala a gaketše
O re tswaletše melomo
O re tswaletše tlabego
O tswala go feta lešikišiki
O naba go feta motšhatšha se enya magapu

O re fetošitše botšhikanoši tšhwene ya roto
Re tšhaba le mamane re a tswetse
Botšhabelo ga re nabjo

O tsebja ke mang?
Badumedi a kgwadi ya boMateo e reng?
A marapo makokonwa ke dimpša ona a reng?
A Baetapele le reng?
O phoofolo mang e kwametšago mere kamoka?
Boela pitšeng re kwele hle!

O re amogile Morekereke a Lebotsa
Tau pheta ya thaga e sa boga molala
Bana ba Sekhukhune re gakilwe ke mogobo
O reng wa re bolotša leboelela?
Ra re re naba maoto, wa re lomiša maritagane

O iphetošitše naletšana
O bolelwa le ke masea a maabane
O reng wa ikuta?
Bonala re bope dipopolwane
Re bone ka dingwathameratha gore poo ke mang
O reng wa hloya merafe kamoka
A o lengeloi go tlo re ruta sengwe?
Go ba o apeilwe boka thothotho?

YOU ARRIVED
Mmabore Gladys Mogashoa

You arrived while us children of Thulare were still rubbing our eyes
We heard rumours about you
That a conqueror is still on the other side

You arrive and start a bush fire
Upon your arrival you failed to greet
Why are you lawless
Your theft even astounds the Creator
Whose son are you?
You uprooted the strongest
When you chop down the old, with what will we lean?
You do not care
We are lamenting
You alone control the whole world
You are omnipresent though invisible
We met them and prevailed
Conqueror even exhausts scientists

You started a rumour mill
You caused us heavy sleep
News of modern technology leave us heaving a sigh
We can no longer cope

Day after day we go to the cemetery
Does your stomach ever fill up?
You devour a calf and its mother
You are like drizzle on Leolo mountain
Us orphans don't know where you fall
You have become an elephant that steps on us like millipedes
You are enraged like a mountain cobra

You close the gates with fences
You close firms your cousin hunger rages
You shut our mouths
You birthed us bewilderment
You birth more than a scorpion
You spread further than a watermelon plant

Like aged baboons you made us into loners
We are scared of our own offspring
We have nowhere to flee

Who knows you?
What does Matthew tell the faithful?
What do sangoma's bones say about you?
Anything from leaders?
What animal are you that swallows every tree?
We have had enough!

You took away Morekereke a Lebotsa
Lion, while we loved him
Children of Sekhukhune we are stunned by the crowd
Why take us through that again?
When we stretch our feet you send black ants to bite us

You have become like a shining star
Even yesterday's infants talk about you
Why are you hiding?
Show yourself so we can ululate
So we can battle it out and see who's boss
Why do you hate all races
Are you an angel sent to teach us a lesson?
Or are you brewed wild like *skokian*?

(an English translation by Goodenough Mashego)

I select these three poems for their discourse, their context, their poetic expression and their creativity, not only because they are the only ones which do these. Many do. But they are also a study in poetry and poetic expression, their varied contexts, discourse and also mother tongue choice and their translations; because even 'notes from ratanang tavern' is English translated into English of a context unlike of English.

The anthology as a whole must be in a language laboratory under a South African, African and human history, culture, heritage, language and creativity microscope to determine who actually these South African, African and human poets are in the first place.

We are not objects of history! We are cultural engineers, in search of and shaping a humane cultural context. The poets in this anthology must know that they are social scientists.

They search the past because they must contribute to a liveable present which must inform and form a best future. Their instinct tells them that there are many things which are interconnected, which need to be understood, and which must be engaged with for a rupture away from a very bad past.

Sol Plaatje would be proud of these poets in this sequence: 'Camagu', 'O Fihlile' and 'notes from ratanang tavern'.

Mongane Wally Serote
June 2021

IPENI LISA PHAKAMA…
Thansanqa Milungisi Cindi
(Zulu)

Ngizwa izinyoni zishaya umlolozi
Ngizwa umculo wase mazulwini,
Ngibona iSibhakabhaka sihlephuka
Kwathaphuka ulwazi olugeleza njengoThukela…

Bengisacela umhlahla'ndlela
Ngaphambi kokuthi nginhlanhlathe,
Bengisacela indlebe
Ngimemezele ezizweni zonke
Njengo Jesu…

Abantu bakithi baphila isilungu
Bakhuluma isilungu
Bathandaza umlungu,
Ingabe iyofundwa yini lena eyami
Inkondlo engasona islungu…

Ngiyayibonga impucuko
Uma isiphuca amasiko,
Idlwengule nolwimi lwethu
Ukuhlukumezeka kwethu
Kuyinjabulo kithi…

#ImbongiEbukhali
#ImbongiEngalali

THE PEN STILL RISES...
Thansanqa Mlungisi Cindi

I hear birds whistle
I hear music of the heavens,
I see the sky breaks up
Then knowledge like Thukela river flows...

I was still asking for guidelines
Before I go astray,
I was still asking for an ear
So I can shout out for all to hear
Like Jesus...

Our people are leading a white man's lifestyle
They speak a white man's language
They pray to a white man,
I wonder if mine will be read
A poem that is not in a white man's language...

I shun sophistication
If it takes away our traditions,
Rapes our language
Our harassment
Is pleasure to us...

#Thefiercebard
#Thenonsleepingbard

Translated from the Zulu original – Ipeni Lisa Phakama... – *by Innocentia Mhlambi*

TO SAVE A COUNTRY
Connor Shay Cogill

One summer there was a mulberry tree
which sprouted suddenly in the backyard heavy
with fruit spilling black into the dirt and foliage.
I sat and gorged myself in the cool shadowy corner
until my hands were purple, until summer left
and with it took the mulberry tree, shrivelled away
to nothing but stains of its sweet dark bearings.

One summer I read a book
about a little boy lost in North America
and I wondered if I was like him, only in Africa –
I have a bad habit of making things about myself
even now as the Cape Town wind bays (as it does)
and I convince myself that it is me it is reviling, me
the centre of all things, the one with the purple hands

who dreams of abandon, who dreams
of the dream house, windproof and on an island.
Not Africa, not America. Just some nameless place
lush with mulberry trees. In this way I am a deserter,
even before I have deserted. Forgive me.
I only wish to gorge myself again
and for the purple not to be blood.

This summer we buy food
then drive down to watch the sunset at Blouberg.
I am keenly aware that this is larger than myself.
The face of my best friend during our last goodbye
before he went back to Zimbabwe. As we watch

the waves collapse. As I wonder what is to be found here.
Besides houses which are merely windows

and the same perversions as every other place, no
exception. But You have raised me – this is personal.
One summer I woke, and the mulberries weren't sweet
anymore. I shut my eyes and feel the earth move.
Questions staining my hands. To run or to save?
Is there saving in this at all? As small as I am?
The child beneath the mulberry tree?

STONES AND FEATHERS
Christine Coates

This summer we had to stay home
with the old things we've become so used to
we hardly see them anymore. The doorstop
burst its seam, I had to bar the sand spilling out.

I walked to the deserted beach to fetch
more sand for the doorstop. I spent time
balancing stones until I'd built a little cairn.

The next day I placed another pebble on top.
It looked like a person, the shape of a woman.
A black bird, a crow, sat there and I thought
they somehow went together.

These opposites; she pale granite, stolid, heavy,
he, shimmering black, tried to sing but
there were feathers in his throat.

They seemed happy, she anchored there,
he flitting in and out, turning his head
this way and that, to hear death passing by.

MAMMIE
Florence Diana De Vries
(Afrikaans)

Mammie't gesê
as jy ná die son sak
waatlemoenpitte eet
gaanit in jou maag loop sit
en tussen jou derms wortel skiet

Mammie't gesê
aunty Carol is 'n krummel wat brood geraakit
want hulle't saam as kinders met appelkose gesmous
en nou ry aunty Carol 'n Merc
en hou vi' ha blind in Woolworths

Mammie't gesê
almal het hulle idiosyncrasies
en die Leviete voorgelees
oor respek vir groot mense
soos oom Daantjie Vuilhol

Mammie't gesê
vroeg ryp, vroeg vrot en
toetie-wawyd meisies gaan sommer
vinnig hulle gat sien
sonder 'n spieël

Mammie't gesê
'n vrou hoefie kos te leer maak nie
sy moet net uie in die pan braai
want dan ruik dit darem soos huis
terwyl sy haar stuk kyk

Mammie't gesê
daar is net een Gebod
met 'n belofte
en soos dinge nou lyk
weet sy darem nie of ons baie lank gaan lewe nie

MOMMY
Florence Diana de Vries

Mommy said
if you eat watermelon
seeds after sunset
they'll get stuck in your tummy
and take root in your intestines

Mommy said
Aunty Carol is a crumb that turned into bread
they used to sell apricots together as children
but now Aunty Carol drives a Merc
and pretends she's blind in Woolworths

Mommy said
everyone has their idiosyncrasies
she called us on the carpet
about respecting our elders
like Uncle Daantjie Dirtass

Mommy said
soon ripe, soon rotten and
girls with open legs will
soon see their ass
without a mirror

Mommy said
a wife doesn't need to cook
she can just fry onions in the pan
so at least it can smell like home
while she watches her soaps
Mommy said

there is only one Commandment
with a promise
and by the looks of things
she's not so sure if we'll live very long

Translated from the Afrikaans original – Mammie – *by Pieter Odendaal*

BROOD EN TEE
Kimberley Elana Fray
(Afrikaans)

Bruinbrood met botter gesmeer.
'n Bietjie bruinsuiker vir die Rooibostee.
Vou die snytjie en dip in die tee.
Dis al wat ons eet van die kaste is leeg.

Die tee maak die sluk makliker,
Krimmels lê op die kas,
As jy honger is proe alles smaakliker.

Die dou breek af in die tee,
Skep dit uit met die teelepel en
dit verdwyn af in my keel.

Chip oppie koppie,
Die teaspoon op die piering.
Dis my favourite koppie,
Gekraak deur my ou toppie.

Mixed fruit jêm of die apricot jêm,
'n warme bord kos is ons enigste wens.

Vir breakfast, lunch en aandete,
Eet ons onse brood en tee,
Ons kla nie,
Ten minste is ons mae nie leeg

My favourite is twee snytjies peanut butter en jêm
3-hoekig gesny
Albany of Blue Ribbon,

My ma verkies eintlik Albany
Sy sê altyd dit last langer.
Wie worry eintlik
As al wat jy aan dink is jou honger?

Daar is 'n bietjie Kellogg's, maar nie melk nie.
"Eet dit, maar met water,"
Sê Ma.
Wie gaan eet en wie gaan kyk?

Daar was altyd brood in ons huis,
My ma het my dit geleer.
Van wanneer die kaste leeg is
Kan ons darem eet,
Al is dit net brood en tee.

BREAD AND TEA
Kimberley Elana Fray

Butter spread on brown bread.
A bit of brown sugar for the rooibos tea.
Fold the slice and dip it in the tea.
It's all we have coz the cupboards are empty.

The tea makes it easier to swallow,
Crumbs lie on the cupboard,
Everything tastes better when you're hungry.

The dough breaks down in the tea,
Scoop it out with a teaspoon and
it disappears down my throat.

The cup is cracked,
The teaspoon on the saucer.
It's my favourite cup,
My old man chipped it.

Mixed fruit jam or apricot jam,
all we want is a warm plate of food.

For breakfast, lunch and dinner
We eat our bread and tea,
We don't complain,
At least our stomachs aren't empty.

My favourite is two slices peanut butter and jam
Cut into triangles
Albany or Blue Ribbon,

My mom prefers Albany
She always says it lasts longer
Who really cares
When the only thing you can think of is your hunger?

There's a bit of Kellogg's, but no milk.
"Eat it, but with water,"
Mom says.
Who will watch and who will eat?

We always had bread at home,
My mom taught me that.
So that we have something to eat
when the cupboards are empty,
Even if it's just bread and tea.

Translated from the Afrikaans original – Brood en Tee – *by Pieter Odendaal*

MOSADI GARE GA BASADI
Kgalalelo Lebogang Gaebee
(Setswana)

Ke mosadi gare ga basadi
Ba bantsi ba mo bitsa mofumagadi
Le fa tota loso lo mo fetotse motlhologadi
Ga aka a tlhanogela ba bogadi

Ke mosadi gare ga basadi
Le fa botshelo bo kile jwa mo sotla
Gwa nna thata, ba bantsi ba seka ba tlhola ba mo tlotla
Ga aka a ineela mathata
Ga aka a fela maatla
O tsweletse go itshwara ka thata

Ke mosadi gare ga basadi
Ga a busi bosula ka bosula
Le fa tota batho ba mo rumula
O dula a ba lakaletsa pula
Gore Keresete a ba gopole motlhang a rula

Ke mosadi gare ga basadi
Le fa tota sekolo a sa se fetsa
A ka go tlhaba botlhale, wa sala mathe o a metsa
Botlhale jwa gawe ke jwa tlhago
Ga se moagi mme a ka go bolelela go le gontsi ka kago
A go fe kitso ka tsa maobane le isago
A go fe maele ka botshelo jwa gago

Ke mosadi gare ga basadi!

WOMAN OF VIRTUE
Kgalalelo Lebogang Gaebee

She's a woman of virtue
Most people call her Missus
Though death turned her into a widow
She stayed loyal to her in-laws

She's a woman of virtue
Though brutalised by life
It was hard, many people stopped giving her respect
She never threw in the towel
She never lost hope
She continued to carry herself with decorum

She's a woman of virtue
Doesn't repay cruelty with the same currency
Even when provoked
She wishes her adversaries well
For Christ to remember them when he rises from the tomb

She's a woman of virtue
Though she didn't finish her school
She can still riddle you, and leave you salivating
She possesses organic wisdom
Notwithstanding not a builder she still knows enough
about architecture
Gives you hints about history and the future
And advise you about your own life

She's a woman of virtue!

Translated from the Setswana original – Mosadi Gare Ga Basadi – *by Goodenough Mashego*

NAKO E FITLHILE
Kgalalelo Lebogang Gaebee
(Setswana)

Nako e fitlhile
Nako ya go tshameka e ile
Lehatshe ba le tshotse o le lebile
Ka ntata ya go utlwa ka tsa ga morakile

E rile maloba wa maabane re reeditse
Wa opa mokgosi re santse re itheeditse
Wa re raya wa re ka Mosupulogo wa ntlha wa Lwetse,
O letse o lorile borra-rona ba re tenenegetse
Ba tenegetse gore rona jaaka setshaba re iketlile

Re robile sogo, e bile re inetse
Ga re ikoke, re balwetsi
Re itlogeletse
E bile jaaka setshaba, re itebetse
Gonne re ithaya re re tiro e weditswe
Tse re neng re di lwela, re di filtheletse
Ruri re iteile se foletse
Ruri re ntse re itsietsa
Borra-rona ba bua le rona, reetsa
Ga ra tswelelela ka ditiro tse ba neng ba sa difetsa

Bona jaanong, dintlo di a nela ga re kgone go beeletsa
Malwetsi le o ne ke a, aa re heketsa
Re lebetse ka lewatle, re lwanela letsha
Re lebetse ka lehatshe re lwanela setsha
Borra-rona ba bua le nna le wena, ba tsee tsia
Motho wetsho, tlogela go sia sia
Se ise pelo mafisa

Wa tlatlhlola pitsa e ntse e fisa
Wa ja dijo o sa di fodisa
Wa tlhanola direthe, wa sia
Borra-rona ba re mphemphe o a lapisa
Ba re re ikemele, re tlogele go itisa

O ineile naga, go lekane
O tshetse botshelo jwa gago o sekame, go lekane
Ke nako ya gore tumelo ya gago e tsepame
Mathata ke a, a re lebane
A re nne ngata ngwee, re kopane
Botshelo ga bona bo re feketsa, a re lwane
Nako e fitlhile
A sediba se sa tsha re se lebile

IT'S TIME
Kgalalelo Lebogang Gaebee

It's time
To stop playing
They conquered the land while you watched
Through ignorance

Day before yesterday while we listened
While lost in our thoughts you shrieked
You said on the first Monday of the month of September,
You dreamt our ancestors are disappointed with us
Disappointed that our nation is relaxed

We have relaxed, and surrendered
We are not healing ourselves, we are ill
We have thrown in the towel
We have forgotten ourselves as a nation
Lying to ourselves that the job is done
That we have gained all we fought for
We tricked ourselves
We are misleading ourselves
Our forefathers are talking to us, listen
We have not finished what they started

Look now, our houses are flooding we can't stop the leaks
We are being chopped down by diseases
We forgot about the sea, we fight for a lake
We forgot about the land, we fight for a site
Our ancestors are talking, pay attention
Please stop wasting time
Don't worry

Don't be too hasty
Avoid jumping the gun
And run away, fleeing
Our fathers say we can't beg forever
They say we should rise, and stop watching out

You wandered, it's enough
You lived a bended life, it's enough
It's time for your focus on faith
We are facing real problems
Let us be one, and unite
When life overpowers us, let us fight
Now is the time
Let a well not dry out while we watch

Translated from the Setswana original – Nako e Fitlhile – *by Goodenough Mashego*

II-V-I
Mamodiehi Gwala

He drowns the weekday strain in the blues,
Playing a ballad II-V-I,
Clipping a stray note on the loyal piano.

Friday nights, torrent with bliss,
Glazed legs hammer an ambiguous pulse,
On a lava dance floor.

Fingers flutter on hood rat keyboards,
Itching for grace notes and glissandos,
A perfect antidote for a honky-tonk piano.

NOT YET UHURU
Bhekumuzi Christopher Kubheka

It's not that a heart doesn't know what it wants.
It's not that our parents didn't fight hard for this country.
It's not that we are being fooled by the so-called viruses.
It's not that we didn't do our best to protect and prevail.
The pandemic is real.
I have lost so many and so did you by this so-called virus.
This is not a child's play, when the cow comes back home with a bell on its neck
It's time to gather all we can and be behind closed doors for the virus lurks all over

BOTHATA BA HAO KENG?
Thabiso Tsietsi Lakajoe
(Sesotho)

Ha o dudisehe, ha o tshwarehe!
Ha o rapelehe, ha o kgalemelehe!
Ha o thapisehe, ha o mamele!
Hantle-ntle bothata ba hao keng?

O fihla kajeno, hosane o a tsamaya!
O a hloma, o hlomolle.
O ikentse thuube ha ena tsatsa,
Ruri o a makatsa.

Mamela mona he thope,
O nkutlwe, o nkutlwisise!
Bohlanyanyana bona ba hao bo tlamehile ho fela,
O ntubisa thankga.

Ke kgathetse ke ho bua ka pelo,
Pelo ya ka e ntsho, e a nyeka.
Boroko ha ke bo hlothe,
Bohadi ba hao o bo fetotse tshehlo.

Bonna ba ka o bo nyenyefaditse!
Pelo ya ka e a sisa,
Ke phela ka ho kgwahlapisa.
Ke kgathetse ke ho qeka,

A ko tlohelle ho nteka tumelo.
Ke tsoha ka dialla
Ke o tsoma sa tjhelete,
Eta tsa ka di bonwa ka phoka le boputswa.

Di se di ile ka lekeke,
Ke hlajwa ke meutlwa. Lebaka ke wena.
O dutse o tshepisa ho boya.
Ha ke o fumana o mpolella hore o tla kgutla.

Maoba o siile mekotlana ya teke e ahlame!
O nahana hore o senatla, athe o sematla.
na ha ke sa batla, o tla tlameha ho kgutla,
Kapa o dule, o dulele ruri. Seja monna ha se mo qete!

WHAT IS YOUR PROBLEM?
Thabiso Tsietsi Lakajoe

You are restless, you are uncontained!
You can't be begged, you accept no advice!
You can't be softened, you don't listen!
Actually, what is your problem?

You arrive today, tomorrow you are gone!
You pitch, and dismantle
You are a rat that never settles,
Indeed you are surprising

Here's a secret for you,
Listen to me, and understand!
Your little madness should cease,
You cause me problems

I'm tired of silently complaining,
My heart is tormented, it's nauseating
I can't even sleep,
You turned your marriage into gossip

You insulted my manhood!
My heart is raging,
I live through gleaning
I'm tired of begging

Please stop testing my faith.
I wake up before dawn
To try and make a living,
My shoes are only seen by dew and frost.

They are old and torn,
I am pierced by thorns. Because of you
You always promise to come back.
When I find you, you promise to return.

Yesterday you left bags open
Thinking you are strong, but you are stupid
I want nothing to do with you, you have to return,
Or stay, and stay forever. You can never exhaust my resolve!

Translated from the Sesotho original – **Bothata Ba Hao Keng?**
– *by Goodenough Mashego*

MOHANUA
Thabiso Tsietsi Lakajoe
(Sesotho)

Moya wa hao o marantha,
O kgeswa ke bao o nyantseng letswele le bona
Ha ba batle ho o bona ka mahlo,
Ba o lwantsha sa ntja le katse,
Mello o e qobile, ya ba ya o tela,
Ha e o bona e a tima,
O thuswa feela ke dithapelo.

Fatsheng lena ha se habo motho,
Bahaeno ba na le wena.
Ba tla o pepa ka mapheo a ntsu,
Tlohella ba keledi tsa kwena,
Ba llang ka leihlo le le leng.
Bahaeno tsela ba tla e betla.
Se ke wa hetla, wa iketsa mosadi wa Lota.

Ditlhabela mme re tla di oka.
Tshehlana phelo bona ke lebidi,
Tsela o a e bona, hole le haufinyana.
Rwala mafolofolo maotong,
mona re leetong hata ka matla.
Tlama sebete thekeng, o intshe seretseng.
Matla ke a hao tiisetsa ho tla loka.

THE REJECTED ONE
Thabiso Tsietsi Lakajoe

Your spirit is in tatters,
Torn by your own siblings
They don't want to see you,
They hound you like cat and mouse,
You avoided fires, until they
When they see you they blow out
Only prayers carry you through.

This world is nobody's home
Your kin are with you
They will carry you on the wings of an eagle
Leave those with crocodile tears,
Who cry with one eye
Your people will pave you a way
Don't lose hope like Lot's wife.

Your wounds we shall heal
Life is a merry-go-round
From far and near, you can see the way
Be quick on your feet,
increase your pace on this journey
Be brave, pull yourself out of slime
With the power in you, all shall be fine.

Translated from the Sesotho original – Mohanu – *by Goodenough Mashego*

ZWA MISHUMONI
Tshindane Livhuwani
(Tshivenda)

Lo tsha ndi mupfufhi u si mphire,
Nwana u mamela Iurumbu,
Vhathu vhe ri ya mishumoni,
Ro tangana rothe ri sa divhani.

Zwa mishumoni zwi koda mirado,
Zwa mishumoni zwi koda mihumbulo,
Wa fara tshila vhe a si zwone,
Wa litsha vhe wo khakha.

Ngavhe ri vhe vho mamaho lithihi,
Mushumo wo vha u tshi do shavha zwanda,
Vhatambi vha nganea vho dala mishumoni,
Fhedzi a vhonalesaho ndi mulutanyi,
Zwone ndi zwa mishumoni.

THE WORKPLACE
Tshindane Livhuwani

As early as the morning sun rise, human beings can be seen moving up and down like fast paced athletes on a racing track.
Indeed, this is sign of people going to work, and everyone having their bags on their backs.
We all walk the same route, and we stand under the same tree-shadow, but still, we do not know each other.

Work drains your energy!!
Working is mentally taxing.
You touch one thing you are reprimanded,
You do not do a certain thing, an offense you have committed.

Our offenses are all the same as if we were brought up by one mother, with all of us sucking milk from the same breast, oh wow, it is tough, it is indeed work.
There are a lot of actors in the workplace,
But the antagonist always finds reasons to shine, he attracts the spotlight.
All these are workplace politics, they are all politics of the workplace, in the workplace you will find all these issues.

Translated from the Tshivenda original – Zwa Mishumoni – by Neo Sehlanhla

TRIMETHYLAMINE
Alinaswe Lusengo

the rotting fish
the sour smell of a country
where men learn how to rape
from their president

the police station is a freezer
the aluminum foil
hoping the layers of ice will
preserve the animal
but knowing the stench remains

it does not leave any corner untouched
wafting through the rooms of children,
sneaking into the post office
and lingering in the homes of women just trying to stay
alive

there is a sort of delirium
that comes from rotting flesh
which might explain why men act the way they do
in this country

which might explain why,
when reporting the sexual assault of my friend,
the police officer asked for my number
and told us how beautiful we looked

the head of the fish blames the tail for its misdirection
but we all know how the saying goes:

a fish rots from the head
or at least Khwezi understood what this meant
when she watched her uncle being sworn into the highest
office

how much louder does death have to be?
how obvious the scent?
will they wait until we all suffocate,
until violence has outdone oxygen
and no one can remember the smell of fresh air?

THE MEMORIES OF VIOLENCE
Zama Madinana

inside this pub
dark confessions ooze like pus
& rusted tables dance with broken legs

to the music of breaking
beer bottles

while cruel fingers
wield burning cigarette stubs
to defenceless ashtrays
every friday
night

bloodstains are memories
of violence
hanging
on the walls
feeding us concrete fear

okapi peeps through
tsotsi's back pocket

& the boys from emcitsheni
carry embers of violence
in their eyes after a bottle of 1818

here floors burp castle lager baba wami

NOTES FROM RATANANG TAVERN
Zama Madinana

they
come here

with scabs
they cannot sing

to wash
their rusted past
in the waters of babylon

they come here
to close
their spiritual abyss

the sick
the poor
& the broken

they soak
tavern walls
in swamps of semen

floods of urine
taunt no man
here

yelling armpits
halt
no tot

of vodka
clouds of ganja smoke
cloak & choke
no laughter
here

here we dodge
flying bricks
& beer bottles
even
the blobs of vomit
cannot tame
the drunken feet
from dancing
to the maskanda rhythms

but songs
of hope-erosion
continue to rape black dignity

how do you escape
a carnage of dreams

in a community of nervous ambitions

IMFAZWE YEZIYOBISI
Landisile Magwaxaza
(Xhosa)

Yimfazwe le madoda,
Yimfazwe efuna zonk'izizwe,
Ziphakame kunye zime ngenyawo
Ziphakame zilwe elidabi
Ziphakame zilwe obu bubi
Imfazwe yeziyobisi yeyona mfazwe.

Ulutsha lwakokwethu luyaphalala,
Abazali nabo beyele.
Bonke bayantyumpantyumpeka,
Baya ntyumpantyumpeka kweli qula.
Iqula elinyhukunyhuku,iqula leziyobisi.
Imfazwe yeziyobisi yeyona mfazwe.
Sonke sinoxanduva,
Uxanduva lokuthetha kuvakale,
Sithethe ngobu bubi singoyiki,
Sithethe ngobu bubi singathengi buso
Sithethe sonke sinyevulel'iziyobisi
Imfazwe yeziyobisi yeyona mfazwe.

Ye! Madoda liyatshon'ilanga
Ye madoda siyaphel'isizwe
Silinde ntoni singaquli siye nje?
Makuyiwe madoda makuyiwe
Elidabi lelethu sonke
Imfazwe yeziyobisi yeyona mfazwe.

Abashishina ngazo mabanqakulwe
Banqakulwe baziswe phambi kwengalo yomthetho

Batshutshiswe, batshutshiswe
Babekw'ityala kuba banetyala
Ityala elingaka, ityala lokubulal'isizwe
Mabagwetyw'abenzi bobubi mabagwetywe
Imfazwe yeziyobisi yeyona mfazwe

Emva kwesigwebo kuyakutsho kuvel'ukukhanya,
Kaloku wonk'amaxhob'aletyhefu
Akuphakama kunye avuthulule
Avuthulule aziphuthume abuyel'endimeni,
Achile achethuzele kude iziyobisi
Ndinga ndingakho ngaloo mhla ndizokubancedisa
Zekube njalo!!!

WAR ON DRUGS
Landisile Magwaxaza

Men this is war
It is a war that needs all nations
To stand up
To stand up and fight this war
To stand up and fight this sickness
The war on drugs is an important war

Our youth is dying
And the parents have gone
They are wallowing
They are wallowing in this mess
A mess of drugs
The war on drugs is an important war
We all have a responsibility
The responsibility to speak up
Speak about the ugly plague with no fear
Speak about this plague without sugar-coating
All of us should speak in disgust
The war on drugs is an important war

Hey! Men the sun is setting
Hey! Men the nation is under attack
What are we waiting for not attacking?
Let's go men let's go
This is our battle all of us
The war on drugs is an important war

Those who trade drugs should be stopped
They should be stopped and brought before the law

They should be prosecuted
They should be convicted if they are guilty
A big case like a case killing a nation
The wrongdoers should be prosecuted
The war on drugs is an important war

After they are prosecuted light will shine
All the victims of this poison
Will get up and dust themselves off
They will dust themselves off and go back to their lives
And move and stay away from drugs
How I long to be there on that day to help them
Let it be so!

Translated from the Xhosa original – **Imfazwe Yeziyobisi** – *by Innocentia Malambi*

LEBOKO
James Mahlangu
(Setswana)

Ruri ke ikutlwa ke robegile moweng
Buka le pene baakanya ke a inela
Ke inela pokong ke tlogela maikutlo
Ke bulela modumo go tlisa tshenolo le tharabololo
Boithumelo rena go nna
Ke tlatse matlhare ka moribo le morethetho
Wa puo gae ke raya sona Setswana

Sedila maikutlo ame mme o dire tsela yame e nne e tlhomameng
Tlogela thata jaaka tlogelo sekapuo
Neeletsana ka mafoko
Mafoko a a tla fetolang matshelo a batho
Mme a nne jaaka tswina e rokotsang mathe
Go tlhotlheletsa tirisano mmogo le lorato mo bathong
Fela jaaka motshishi wa dinotshe

Wena o tla nthusang go fapoga mathata
Ka go mpaya lofelo le le lengwe
O mpaya lefelong le ke ikutlwang ke phuthulogile
Ke le gare ga ntlu le buka le pene
Ka go itshireletsa ke tla dira bonye jwame
Kgatlhanong le ntwa ya kokwanatlhoko Khorona

POEM
James Mahlangu

I feel my soul is tormented
Book and pen I surrender myself
Surrender to praise and leave emotion
I unleash sound to bring revelation and solution
Happiness prevail in me
Fill pages with rhythm and blues
Of Setswana my home language

Illuminate my feelings and straighten my path
Abandon excessively like a figure of speech
Share words
Words that will change people's lives
And be like honey that will make you salivate
To encourage love and working together among people
Like a colony of bees

You who will help me evade troubles
By finding another place for me
Put me in a place where I will find peace
In a house with a book and a pen
To protect myself I will do my part
Against the coronavirus

Translated from the Setswana original – Leboko – *by Goodenough Mashego*

LORATO
James Mahlangu
(Setswana)

Lorato ke netse bojotlhe go wena
Wena letlhafulo ke tla kutulang seleng tshimong
Peo e e jadilweng ke batho babedi
Go tseediwa ke motlho mmung
Ya nna yona kgaogano ya baratani

Bosetlhogo jo bo phalang tshego ya thipa
Nako ngwe le ngwe ke go gakologelang
Tshetlho e tlhaba pelong
Dikgomo di tla lala nageng
Ke itumileng sankatlhe kere bo malome ke a mo nyala
Di tlatsang losaka kwa gaeno jaaka o ntladitseng boitumelo

Tota mokapelo wame o ntirileng wa ntatlha lesa phirima
Le dibeke di ese di wele wa ntemosa bokhukhuni jwa gago
Ga o swabe ke eng?
Ka go bega badimong mme ka ikana goya lwena lesong
O itirile tolla ka kgatlhwa ke bontle jwa mmala wa gago
Jaanong ke metsa mateng a yona

Fa ke tshegiwa ke banna motseng
Ke tla lelela kae mme metsi a dilelo tsame a tla tlatsang dinoka
Dinoka di tla elelang goya go ile go phala lorato la gago
Lorato le le sa felelang gope
La felela mo dikobong tsa tsala yame
Nkutlwelela ke a tshologa ka sefako ke a lela
Ka fa lerato le botsalano jwa nnete bo le jwa bogologolo

LOVE
James Mahlangu

To you I gave all my love
You Autumn what shall reap that I planted in the field
A seed planted by two people
To be cheated by termites on the ground
That's how the lovers went separate ways

Cruelty worse than a cut from a knife
Everytime I miss you
A thorn pierces my heart
Cattle are left wandering unattended not coming home
I bite my elbow told my uncles I am marrying her
That filled your homestead's kraal as you filled me with pride

What did my partner do dumping me before sunset
In less than a few weeks you showed me your treachery
Have you no shame?
I reported you to my ancestors and swore to eternally love you
You became a wild berry your bright complexion
fascinated me
Today I swallow its bitter nectar
As other men laugh at me

Where shall I cry where my tears will fill rivers
Rivers that unlike your love will flow forever
Love that ended nowhere
It ended on my friend's bed
Listen as I cry a hail of tears
When true love with companionship is a thing of the past

Translated from the Sepedi original – Lorato – *by Goodenough Mashego*

WEDDINGS AND FUNERALS
Nolwazi Mbali Mahlangu

An augury hangs
In the clouds of our closet.
The weather stretches its arms
And folds my husband
Into a nomad.
A stray animal.
My husband draws
A map on my skin.
Makes a plan to travel
Out the front door.
This wardrobe
Against the wall is for
The married and marred.

The ritual is the same.
And so is everyone.
An Ezekiel
A sangoma
Everything made of prophecy and bones.

We are their ribs
Wear these body bags as skin.
And with every blow
We get thrown onto deserted streets.
Ke ge e le bonkadingala.
We are compasses
For men who try
To find themselves outside their homes.

We are Saul

Soul searching in streams
We've thrown our backbones
Bending backwards to build bridges.
Blooming;
This is how we bring
Our marriages back to life.

GE NKABE O LE GONA
Tshepiso Makgoloane
(Sepedi)

Ke sokolela'ng o le gona?
O reng wa nkotla ka bokgopo bja mma wa ka?
Ke sentše'ng ge lehono ke hwela melato ya gagwe?
Phelong bja ka ke tšhešerekano, ga go na tšwelopele
Meloko e fošetšana ka nna boka kgwele-ntlatlana
Ka ge mma a ikgapa a ikgoroša,

A fetola maisa boka mengato ya ka gare.
Maikarabelo ke phophoma ka a go mpheta
A nkgama, a ntshwere ka megolo
Ga ke sa kgona go buša moya, go boima go nna.
Khutšo monaganong ke e duma e feta ka tsela.
Tate o reng o ntlhobogile ke sa buša moya?

O reng o ntlogetše etšwe le wa ka molomo o sa o tsebe.
Ge bohle ba mpotšiša ka wena, ke reng?
Ke ba botše gore o ragile lepai goba o kae?
Ke a botšiša ka ge ke apere kgakanego.
Mmemotswadi o mpotapota ka therešo,
Go bohloko go nna, ke ralala le naga,

Ke ebela le mekgotha ke se na lesedi.
Ge bangwe ba ikgantšha ka botate
Nna ke inamiša hlogo boka nku ge e ekwa letšatši
Ya ba ke kgabakgabiša dikgobe ka pelobohloko.
Ka kgopolo ye imetšwego ke maima le dipotšišo.
Afa ge o bintšha mogolo, o a nkgopola?
Ge tša matlorotloro di tšhologa, o nkgopola?
Ge bangwe ba bolela ka matswiana bona, wena o reng?

Ka mogau wa Gagwe ke godile
Ke ka moo ke sa go nyakelego go tlo nkgodiša,

Tumo ya ka ke ge nka bonana le wena
Ke go botšiše potšišwana tše pedi serokaphatla
Gore o ntlogeleng,
O reng o nkotla ka bokgopo bja mma wa ka.

IF YOU WERE HERE
Tshepiso Makgoloane

Why am I suffering while you are here?
Why punish me for the sins of my mother?
What have I done when today I am tormented for her transgressions?
My life is confusion, there is no progress
Relatives use me for their games like I was a soccer ball
Because my mother does it all

She changed men like underwear
I overflow with responsibility
They choke me, holding me by the neck
I can't breath, it's hard on me
I wish for peace of mind which I can't have
Why has my father turned his back on me while I still live

Why abandon me while you've never heard me speak
What should I say when they ask me about you?
Should I say you are dead or where are you?
I ask because I am confused
My mother hides the truth
It's hard on me, I wander around

I walk around the street without light
When others brag about their dads
I bow my head like a sheep exposed to the sun
And I prepare my meals in heartache
My mind weighed down by baggage and questions
Do you remember me when you drink?
When it rains do you remember?

When others talk about their children what do say?

Under His grace I have grown
Which is why I don't want you to raise me

My wish is to meet you
Just to ask you two questions face to face
Why did you leave me
Why punish me for the sins of my mother

Translated from the Sepedi original – Ge Nkabe O Le Gona
– *by Goodenough Mashego*

DIKATA
Charles Julie Makofane
(Sepedi)

Wena dikata, dikata banna
Wena lebake, lebaka tlala.
Batsebi ba gago ba go bitša patše
Ba bangwe ba go bitša mošwang wa matuba.
O reng o itelediša ka matswiana lehono
Mola re tseba o folwa ke banna?

O reng o ba hlokiša boroko
O ba fetotše digatamarokgo?
Gobaneng o ba tladitše mo mabenkeleng
O sa ba khutšiše go re kgopela diponto?
O ba holofeditše eng se sebotse seo re sa se tsebego
Gona o reng o ba lwiša le kwena?

Kgalema dikgaphamamina tše ka bogolo,
O di bontšhe gore o mabelemabutšwa mafolwa ke
bagologolo.

DIKATA
Charles Julie Makofane

You dikata, who conquers men
You tobacco, who causes hunger
Those who know you call you ganja
Others call you mošwang wa matube
Why allow children to disrespect you
While we know you are courted by men?

Why deny them sleep
You have turned them into drunkards?
They fill the shops
And beg us for rands and cents?
What good did you promise them that we know not about
Why make them hate water?

As an elder please warn these kids
Show them you are a rich crop fit for ancestors

Translated from the Sepedi original – Dikata – *by Goodenough Mashego*

RE HLOBOGA PIDIBIDI
Thebogo Patricia Mamabolo
(Sepedi)

Thokwana khutlwaneng ba go beile
Ka lepokisi la go ja boleng bja godimo
O farafarilwe bja bogoši, nkabe o sa phela
Le ntši e be e ka se go kotamele
Ka tatelano ba bapile go se le yo a myemyelago

Ka ponya mahlo motsotswana ka bona pono
E le bophelo bja gago ka moo ke go tsebago
Ke be ke rata go go bogela letamong
O thalathala ka mafofa a gago a go taga
A nkgadimela bja leratadima bošegogare marega
Mphatlalatšane a sa pšhe mathe a ekwa bose
O fela o kobolakobola bogodimo bja meetse
Molodi o tšwago magalagapeng a gago o nkgokakgoketša
Ka gore ke be ke sa laletšwa ke utswa lenna ke ikutile ka lefoka
Ka khupa moya maleng ka itatswa molomo
Go na le matšoba a mebalabala leribeng la letamo
O fela o phurulla diphego ge o fihla kgauswi le ona

Ka hloka setšiadiswantšho go ipolokela mphago
Go bolela nnete lenyora la botse bja gago le fela le ntshwara
Go kgabola wena kgogo ya mabala Pidibidi kgopolong yaka
Moruti Mpša o dutše komana madula a bapile
Ke kgale a leka go go hlothola ka mafofa
A šitišwa ke nna ge ke mmone go nkga lefotha rotlwane ye ya mosela
Ba rile ge ba hlaba mokgoši wa etshwangmare a phallela, lehu ga se sephiri

Ka go longwa ke dibe tša gagwe a kgopela go swara tirelo
Ke mmone kgale pelo e a baba
Ge e le nna ke tlo goga boima letamong o se gona

Matšatši ke a mabedi diatla ke bofilwe ke mešomo ya ka gae
Ge ke boa letamong ka gakanega
Ka fahlwa ke meriti ya diphoofolo go bonagala manyami feela
Go aperwe ka mokgwa wa go se tlwaelege, bao ba lego fao ba a balwa
Go pipilwe dinko le melomo go sena kgohlaganyo ya mmele
E le poloko ya go se tlwaelege lefase le bilogile
Gothwe leuba la bolwetši le aparetše lefase, ga le fete feela
Le tšere sethabiša mahlo aka Pidibidi sekgwari meetsing
Ka hlwaya tsebe go kwa mantšu a Moruti Mpša
O laodiša ka moo twatši ya gona e lego bogale e re hutšego monapelo
Se bohloko ke gore setopo sa gagwe se ka se hlobogwe
Bolwetši gothwe ke "Corona, Covid-19", mogongwe ke mafahla aretse!
Bo ntlapurutseditše mogwera ebile e le sethakga sa go thala letamong
Robala le mebalabala ya gago Nonyana ya potego le maikarabelo
Ke tla kwalakwatša lesolo la go boloka bao ba šetšego
Go re ba ikhurupetše melomo, ba šime ba hlape diatla kgafekgafe
Ba se lebale go šia sekgala ge ba le mafelong a pepeneneng.

WE MOURN A DUCKLING
Thebogo Patricia Mamabolo

You were put in a secluded corner
In an expensive casket
Accompanied like royalty, if you were still alive
Even a fly wouldn't bow down to you
In a procession they file past without smiles

In the blink of an eye I saw a vision
Of your life as I knew it
I loved to watch you at the dam
Swimming with your colourful feathers
Shining like a cloudless sky on a winter night
The morning star not spitting feeling good
Often nibbling at the top of the water
Your glorious melody attracting me
Because I was not invited I was stealing a gaze hiding behind a cane
Held my breath licking my lips
There are colourful flowers on the river bank
You spread your wings when you reached them

I didn't have a camera to archive your pictures
To be honest I miss your beauty
My mind is filled with thoughts of your beauty, you bird of colour Duckling
Pastor Dog is sitting ready for action
He's been trying hard to grab you by the feathers
Only stopped by me seeing through his vile intentions
When they gave the death notice, since death cannot be a secret
Feeling guilty for his sins he requested to conduct the

funeral service
I saw his pain a long time ago
As for me I'll have a hard time without you in the dam

After two days of being busy at home
When I returned to the dam I was amazed
Blinded by shadows of other animals in obvious sadness
The few gathered dressed in unusual garbs,
Mouth and nose covered in masks and social distancing observed
An unusual funeral the world has become a strange place
They say the pandemic is not just a passing fad
It snatched Duckling an expert swimmer who used to enthuse my eye
In anticipation I wait a eulogy from Pastor Dog
He explains how the virus is so contagious it stole our beloved
It's sad that we can't even mourn Duckling's corpse
They call the disease "Corona, Covid-19", it could be tuberculosis!
It took my friend who was an expert swimmer
Rest in your colourful feathers trusted and responsible bird
I will spread the message to spare those who survive you
To wear masks, and wash their hands repeatedly
They must not forget social distancing when in public places

Translated from the Sepedi original – **Re Hloboga Pidibidi** – *by Goodenough Mashego*

MHLABA, MY SON
Maakomele R. Manaka

For you
I cut a new line
forge a different chord
for my ancestral string
to calabash epic streams
for you to claim
as your birthright

& as you meander through
the mountains of manhood
wearing my lineage as your boots
forget not the maternal
marrow in your bones
for it is through our mothers
we can trace our roots

Mhlaba my son
I too know the scent
of disappointment
from my father's clothes
& so I want to
make no promises
but to love you as much
as the poems I wrote

& I hope that some day
my poems will keep you safe
& pay for whatever taste
you want on your plate

but sometimes
I feel helpless & afraid
when I look at the violence
on today's page for you to read
before you come of age

but as a rusting old
automatic from the '80s
that survived every kind
of unkind weather
I'm here for you my son
in you I see the boy I used to be
sweet & sensitive
with a similar silence…
that still recalls
how pain & rage
tore out of me

oh Mhlaba my son
for you
I carve a new star
you can always depend on me
my son, how I wish
I could have met you
at first light
of your first breath
but as a fatherless man
fathering the feathers

of another man's son
I am grateful & thankful
& because of you
I learned to man again
feel no pain when the sun
sleeps on today's hand
for in you is my birthright
the soil in tomorrow's land
land of a child's love
that cannot be replaced
nor erased
but
nurtured

THE LAST STRETCH
Adré Marshall

You led us over mountain peaks, sure-footed
as a klipspringer on the rocks, always stretched
a hand to steady our steps on the steep slopes
or ledges hanging high above the contour path.

February drew us up Skeleton Gorge
to the aqueduct, where you pointed out
red disas, gold-dusted butterflies flaring
silky wings in nests of moss above the stream.

In the Cederberg, we watched with you
as a silver moon briefly shredded
in the skeletal branches of a cedar tree
before slowly gliding across the sky.

Now, you clutch my arm as I walk with you
along the passage of the Sunshine ward.
You've not eaten or spoken for days on end.
Your eyes have sunken deep into your head.

A window opposite shows a scrap of garden
where a bush holds a straggle of blue flowers.
You point at it and I open the window,
before guiding your hand through the space.

Your fingers tremble as you stretch towards
a flower. Your face unfolds. "Ah, the same,
still so soft." You turn to me and I whisper
"Plumbago". The name hovers on your lips
as we walk back on the stretch of lino.

HOME LIKE A TOMB
Keketso Adorn Mashigo

i waken early, and see my mother
rising in the dark.
collect twigs at the back of our rdp house,
put plastic material between the nicely arranged twigs. light
the fire with a match scrapped on the floor emblazoned
with potholes.
then open a fading-yellow 20ltrs bucket,
the bucket is stained with brown from years
of washing it using grains of soil. then measuring
water for trinco tea, and later the smell of cheap
tea coming through. before we eat pap and artchar with the
tea.
i would see her drying
the rusty spoons, opens a broken drawer,
balance it with her knee. then drops them one by one
in the broken drawer bought at maleek,
an indian shop at the corner of our unpaved street.
there is fog at the broken window and it is thickening. i use
my coarse fingers to draw pie before i start eating it
with my imaginary teeth. my stomach groans. but i ignore it
by remembering what those ragamuffins, one of them a
councillor's son, said: "your mother got laid for food
parcels,"
before they chorused a continued laughter.
the no-name brand 5kg rice. the no name brand 12.5kg
mielie meal.
and expired tinned fish. in our yard the young avocado tree,
barely taller than my mother, drops its first avocado. she
listens, and hears nothing – it's a season of food, not empty

promises from politicians.
my mother says before she pushes her wheelchair, it has
a makeshift wheel, back into the ugly rdp glossed with
peeling cheap paint. when it rains we sleep with bath tubs next to
our beds to collect drops of rain. the newsreader
on thobela fm, played on our telefunken broken down stereo,
says the president of the country
plans to eliminate poverty by creating equality –
and my mother sits on her wheelchair wondering where
our next meal will come from.

i sink back to bed. the silence in the house
screams without saying any word. my pillow is cold,
the old odour of m'katabongolo soap still hangs in the air,
my hands are cold – even if i confide to mama that,
themba, the 45 years old spaza-shop owner, repeatedly
rapes me for atchar and few tea bags –
it's not worth it. because even mandla the police officer
repeatedly did it for free anyway!

MADODA KWANELE
Zongezile Matshoba
(Xhosa)

Madoda kwanele
Yini isimbonono esingaka
Kugxizise abazali nezizalwana
Kubhomboloze imibutho yesisa namanina
De kukhale isifundisi sonke nkqu noMongameli welizwe

Yini bafondini
Ninentliziyo ezilukhuni kangaka
Ningenalusizi nalusini kangaka
Yini ukunkaniza ninqandwa de niqine enyaleni
NguSathana nenzondo yantoni le ingaka
Anithunduzelwa na zizijilwi zomama nomntwana
Anihanjelwa ngumzimba na kukuxhaxha umntu ongalwiyo
Aninasazela na kukuthatha umphefumlo womntu ongenatyala
Nilala njani kukho umntu omshiye edunduluzile wamfihla
Niqale nini na ukuba ngumgwebi womntu ongamzalanga
Sanukunkaniza nixelise abafun'utywala buphelile
Sanukuxelis"ootsotsi bephak'inkunzi umntu ongenanto
Ubomi bomntu obhinqileyo ayizoziyobisi ezifunwa nasebumnyameni

Makungade kubhubhe wonke umntu obhinqileyo ukuze niyeke
Phezani, noko kwanele madoda
Abhinqileyo kudala becela amaxolo
PHEZANI!

MEN IT IS ENOUGH
Zongezile Matshoba

Men it is enough
Why so much carnage
Parents and relatives crying aloud
Women's organisations are up in arms
Even the president of the country is crying

Why men
Why are you so hard hearted
Why do you have no mercy
Why are you so stubborn that you stand in shame
Why so much evil and hatred
You are unbothered by the cries of women and children
Your skin does not crawl when hackling a defenceless person
You do not have a conscience when taking the life of an innocent person
How do you sleep knowing that you have hidden a dead body
When did you become the judge to a person that you did not birth
Stop being stubborn like people who want to finish alcohol
Stop being like thieves who mug people that have nothing
A life of a woman is not drugs that are being sought in the dark

Not all women should die until you decide to stop
It is enough now
Women have been begging for forgiveness for a long time now
HOLD IT!

Translated from the Xhosa original – **Madoda Kwanele** – *by* *Innocentia Mhlambi*

KHUTHAZEKA KE BHINQ' ELIHLE
Mzoli Mavimbela
(Xhosa)

Ndikubonil' ukhula ndalozela.
Ndikubonil' uzabalaza ndabukela.
Ndibevile bekubabaza ndangqina
Ndiyaqaphel' uzimisele; qhuba!
Ndibon' ubukhazikhazi; bukhangele.
Ndiv' impumelelw' ikukhweba; yibambe.
Ndithi khula sihlahla wondl' isizwe.
Ngalo mbongo ndithi khanya gqiyazana.
Ubhetele kub' unembeko nentobeko.
Unqwa negush' ukululama: hlal' unjalo.
Uzingqi zingqiyaza kamnandi zibonwe ngezenzo.
Ulizwi limnand' okwamanz' omthombo.
Uz' uxhents' uxhathis' uxube nexhala.
Ube sisibane; intsika nentyatyambo yekhaya.
Uz' uhambe uye ubuye nayw' ekaNobel.
Uz' uhlal' ukhuthazekile ke bhinq' elihle.
Uz' uwatyeshele k' awasebuhlanti kub' akukuhlaba.
Uz' ungevi mntu; ungathembi mntu.
Uz' uthi gqolo uqhuqh' ecaweni.
Uz' uman' undikhweba mhla ngengxaki.
Uz' ubahlonel' abadala uhlale kuloo mendo.
Uz' uval' umlom' uvul' izandla ufunde.
Uz' ungafani nenkcenkc' ekhenkcezayo.
Uhlal' umhle njalo ke mbelukaz' ecwengileyo.
Xa kungekho ban' okuvuyisayo zivuyise.
Xa kungekho ban' okuncomayo zincome.
Zingce, zidle, zithembe, ziwonge.
Zikhuthaze, zithuthuzele, zithande.
Zombelele, ziqhwabele, zithundeze.

Kheth' isiqu sakho ugqibele ngesakhe.
Kheth' ikamva lakho ugqibele ngelakhe.
Sebenza nzima, thandaza ngamandla.
Funda ngokuzinikela, gqwesa, phumelela!
Khuthazeka ke bhinq' elihle uyathandwa!
Be encouraged beautiful woman!

BE MOTIVATED BEAUTIFUL WOMAN
Mzoli Mavimbela

I watched you grow up
I watched you struggle I watched
I heard them speak highly I agreed
I see you are ardent go on
I see glitter, search for it
I see success is beckoning you
I say grow tree and feed the nation
With this poem I say shine bright
You are better because you are respectful and are humble
You are like a sheep stay like that
You are like sails that move nicely
You have a soft voice like a water fountain
You dance with joy and mix it with worry
You are a light a pillar and flower of the home
Go and come back with the Nobel prize
Keep on motivated like that beautiful woman
Be wary of your surrounding as you might be led astray and get pricked
Listen to no one trust no one
Open you eyes wide
Keep on beckoning me when you have a problem
Keep on respecting the elders and stay in your marriage
Close your mouth and open your hands and learn
Do not be like an empty shiny object
Stay beautiful beautiful like that
If the is no one that is making you happy make yourself happy
If there is no one that compliments you, compliment yourself

Be proud of your self, be confident and honour your self
Encourage yourself, comfort yourself,
Beckon yourself, applaud your self
Choose yourself and choose others after
Choose your future and choose his after
Work hard, pray with power
Study by giving it your all success!
Be encouraged beautiful woman!

Translated from the Xhosa original – Khuthazeka Ke Bhinq' Elihle – *by Innocentia Mhlambi*

GRANNY
Frank Meintjies

I wish I'd said
I love you, face to face
Just before the river broke its banks
And swept so much away
But now I need to
Peer at screens, zoom in on eyes
And your newly trimmed hair
As usual, well tugged and clipped
No coffee or tea
Intermittently, you look fuzzier than me
One day, we'll truly unmute
And go for a stroll
In a small garden with occasional bench
There'll be no chat box to filter and strain
These verses to you

BAYAPHI UBUNTU
Mandlakayise Mfanta
(Xhosa)

Sisizukulwan'esinjani na esi,
Siphila njani na kulemihla,
Oxhel'eyakhe akabuzwa,
Kwazenzele akukho ntloni,
Asinqandani siyavulana,
Akukho mntu woyik'ihlazo,
Ngamanyundululu mihla le.
Imibuliso yinkwalambisa,
Uncumo lwethu lelobuxoki,
Impilo siyibuza ngokungakhathali,
Siyibuza sidlula singanakanga,
Nophendulayo akanyaniseki,
Noba segula akazibiki,
Kuba kakade akukho luhoyo.
Nabasweleyo abasaceli,
Kwanabahambi balala phandle,
Babefudula bebelezelelwa,
Kunamhla nje bajongwa nje,
Ebantwaneni kunzinginzingi,
Bekufudula kuqeqeshelwana,
Bekufula kukhuliselwana,
Kodwa kule mihla akusenjalo,
Ndoda nendoda ijong'owayo.
Besifudula sicebisana,
Kulemihla ndijong'okwam,
Besikade sisoluselana,
Kulemihla ndijong'ezam,
Besifudula sincazelana,
Kulemihla utshay'elakho,

Besifudula siphuzisana,
Kulemihla usel'obakho,
Mz'ontsundu inene konakele,
Masibuyelen'eMbo maAfrika.

WHERE HAS HUMANITY GONE
Mandlakayise Mfanta

What generation is thus,
How do we live in these days,
The one who slaughters his own is not questioned,
Everyone does as they please there is no shame,
We do not reprimand one another instead we urge one another on,
There is no one afraid of shame,
It is just shameless acts day in and day out.
Greetings are just a lip service,
Our smiles are just pretense,
We ask after one another's health without care,
We just ask to pass on time without due consideration,
Even the one who responds is not truthful,
Even when sick they do not say,
Because indeed there is no care.
Those without no longer ask for alms,
Even travellers sleep outside,
They used to be catered for,
Today people just stare at them,
Among children it is difficult,
People worked together to train them,
People used to help rear them,
But today it is no longer like that,
Each man looks after his own.
People used to advise each other,
These days I look after my own,
We used to herd for one another,
Today I look after my own,
People worked together and shared among themselves,

Today you smoke what is yours,
People shared beverages,
Today you drink only your own,
House of the black nation, indeed things have gone wrong,
Let us go back to Mbo Africans.

Translated from the Xhosa original – Bayaphi Ubuntu – *by Innocentia Mhlambi*

O FIHLILE
Mmabore Gladys Mogoshoa
(Sepedi)

O fihlile bana ba Thulare re sa ipikitla malaka
Mabarebare re a kwele ka wene
Gore phokgo o sa le ka mošola
O fihla le go tšhuba hlaga
O paletšwe le go tamiša ka mafateng a matelele
O reng wa hloka molao
Bja gago bohodu bo kgotsiša le mmopi
A gona o morwa mang?

O tumutše mekgapa ka medu
A gao swiela a matala digatlela ro ithekga kae?
O pharola metshere
Bana re a golola
O laola lefase ka bophara o le tee
O nabile le ge ka a nama re sa go bone
Re kopane natšo ra di kgona
Phokgo o fegediša le boramahlale
O tsošitše dipolelo
O re swarišitše sekatapowana
Tša mararankodi a sebjalebjale ditaba di re kgebiša segošane
Re sepipamoyeng ga re sa kgona

Tšatši ka tšatši go go iwa mabitleng
A ya gago mpa ga e tlale?
O phura mamane le bommabo
O swana le tsheola thaba Leolo
Ditšhiwana ga re tsebe o wela kae

O iphetošitše tlou o re gata boka magokolodi
O gaketše bo ka mokopa wa thaba

O tswalela difero ka magora
O tswalela mešomo motswalago tlala a gaketše
O re tswaletše melomo
O re tswaletše tlabego
O tswala go feta lešikišiki
O naba go feta motšhatšha se enya magapu
O re fetošitše botšhikanoši tšhwene ya roto
Re tšhaba le mamane re a tswetse
Botšhabelo ga re nabjo

O tsebja ke mang?
Badumedi a kgwadi ya boMateo e reng?
A marapo makokonwa ke dimpša ona a reng?
A Baetapele le reng?
O phoofolo mang e kwametšago mere kamoka?
Boela pitšeng re kwele hle!

O re amogile Morekereke a Lebotsa
Tau pheta ya thaga e sa boga molala
Bana ba Sekhukhune re gakilwe ke mogobo
O reng wa re bolotša leboelela?
Ra re re naba maoto, wa re lomiša maritagane

O iphetošitše naletšana
O bolelwa le ke masea a maabane
O reng wa ikuta?

Bonala re bope dipopolwane
Re bone ka dingwathameratha gore poo ke mang
O reng wa hloya merafe kamoka
A o lengeloi go tlo re ruta sengwe?
Go ba o apeilwe boka thothotho?

YOU ARRIVED
Mmabore Gladys Mogoshoa

You arrived while us children of Thulare were still rubbing our eyes
We heard rumours about you
That a conqueror is still on the other side
You arrive and start a bush fire
Upon your arrival you failed to greet
Why are you lawless
Your theft even astounds the Creator
Whose son are you?

You uprooted the strongest
When you chop down the old with what will we lean?
You do not care
We are lamenting
You alone control the whole world
You are omnipresent though invisible
We met them and prevailed
Conqueror even exhausts scientists

You started a rumour mill
You caused us heavy sleep
News of modern technology leave us heaving a sigh
We can no longer cope

Day after day we go to the cemetery
Does your stomach ever fill up?
You devour a calf and its mother
You are like drizzle on Leolo mountain
Us orphans don't know where you fall

You have become an elephant that steps on us like millipedes
You are enraged like mountain cobra

You close the gates with fences
You close firms your cousin hunger rages
You shut our mouths
You birthed us bewilderment
You birth more than a scorpion
You spread further than a watermelon plant
Like aged baboons you made us into loners
We are scared of our own offspring
We have nowhere to flee

Who knows you?
What does Matthew tell the faithful?
What do sangoma's bones say about you?
Anything from leaders?
What animal are you that swallows every tree?
We have had enough!

You took away Morekereke a Lebotsa
Lion, while we loved him
Children of Sekhukhune we are stunned by the crowd
Why take us through that again?
When we stretch our feet you send black ants to bite us

You have become like a shining star
Even yesterday's infants talk about you

Why are you hiding?
Show yourself so we can ululate
So we can battle it out and see who's boss
Why do you hate all races
Are you an angel sent to teach us a lesson?
Or are you brewed wild like skokian?

Translated from the Sepedi original – O Fihlile – *by Goodenough Mashego*

FOR MY UNCLES (MANDLA AND JABU) IN EXILE
After Ben J. Langa – Staffrider February 1980
Siza Nkosi-Mokhele

all the letters you wrote from exile
how did you send them? because
we never received them

I am writing this poem because
I know that's where I'll find you
here in the poems I write

they didn't know.

mama still talks about the both of you.
Malum' Mandla, I found your children on Facebook
Nomagugu and Themba Maswanganye
we talk. now and then share memories of you
pictures you carried when skipping the country
and the ones we took at your funeral

they were born too far from home
we will welcome them with a goat's bile one day
when history remembers unnamed graves

remember bra Joe? I saw him at a funeral last week
he cried when he saw me, said I remind him of you guys.
apparently the last time he saw you Malum' Jabu
your face was covered in blood. He thought you were dead

your spirits are in these stories.

Sparks died drunk and broke
braWandi runs a restaurant & bnb
other men are limping and stammering
loitering, raising grandchildren

I'm sure Mdu last took a bath in 1982
when amabhunu hit his head with the back of an ak47
he walks around with pieces of his world in plastic bags
he doesn't have an ID and what can we do?

what happened to the spear of the nation
I wonder what was written in your letters
a litany of dead corrupt comrades?

the moon remembers the day you left

when Maponya sold the supermarket to Shoprite
all the spaza shops closed down and the Pakistans took over
it's still rough eDube hostel. they boom ATMs, break into shops
Makhedama is still there. Still sells meat but he's also struggling because of Shoprite. The flower shop is still there
next to the butchery. flowers are shadowed by strands of hair
and litter on the ground

a lot of people you know have died

most neighbours have extended their houses –
3 backrooms and a garage.
the apricot and peach trees are gone
we have broken street lights and street humps

Mlangeni died last year. they gave him a state funeral
the whole army was there
braJoe introduced me to some members
"umshana ka Jabu Bob Marley lo"
their eyes were running
they attended to their drinks

Soweto can't afford electricity
people write their names down for food parcels

you loved this country so much that you left it
can you believe that Tokyo married ingamla and left Dube
I used to see his mother at Fatima
the time I attended mass every Sunday

I no longer go to church
there's an unsettling whiteness inside its walls
I am centring my calling
I am writing this poem

I now stay in Kimberly
and refuse to speak Afrikaans

LEFU LA MORENA HINTSHA KA 1835
Tsela Jeffrey Moloi
(Sesotho)

Jo nna! Manyesemane le ne le le sehloho.
Le ne le bolaya mofutsana le morenae.
Masole a manyesemane le ka re jwetsa hore le ne le
mmolayelang Morena Hintsha.
Wena Harry Smith ba ne ba o tlotla ka dife ha ba ne ba re o
monghadi?
E le hobane o lwanne ntweng ya Waterloo kgahlanong le
Napoleone?
Ebe ba ne ba o romele mona Aforika hore o tlo iketsetsa
borata?
Ke eng seo o neng o se tsekisa Morena Hintsha?
E ne e le hobane a ne a hana ka lefatshe la setjhaba sa hae?
Hobaneng ha le ne le bitsa Morena Hintsha, le mo thetsa
hore o tla sireletseha ha a fihla kampong ya lona?
Hobaneng ha le ne le mo kwetela le mo etsa motshwaruwa?
O ne a le kolotang eo le ne le batla hore a e patale dikgomo
tse mashome a mabedi a metso e mehlano ya dikete?
Wena Harry Smith, hobaneng ha o ne o noanyetsa
Morena o mo theola pereng ya hae hore makwala a heno a
mmolaye?
Ha o ne o laela hore makwala a heno a mo kgaole hlooho e
ne e le ka mabaka afe?
Mora enwa wa Xhotseng ha le ne le mmolaya ka sehloho
jwalo ka nyamatsane e be molato e ne e leng?
Hobaneng ha o ne o re ya tla o tlisetsang ditsebe tsa
mohale enwa o tla mo putsa ka jwala?
Jo nna! Mofumahadi Victoria, wa tle wa se tshepa sekweta
sena sa hao.

THE DEATH OF HINTSA IN 1835
Tsela Jeffrey Moloi

Yooo! You English were cruel
You were killing the poor and his king
Can the English army tell us why they killed King Hintsa
As for you Harry Smith why did they call you Sir?
Was it because you fought against Napoleon at Waterloo?
Then they sent you to Africa to do as you please?
What was your challenge against King Hintsa?
Is it because he was refusing to hand over the land of his people?
Why did you summon and deceive King Hintsa that he will be safe at your camp?
Why did you capture and make him prisoner?
What did he owe you that had to be settled with twentyfive thousand herds of cattle?
Why did you Harry Smith creep behind the King and pull him from his horse for your cowards to murder him?
When you instructed your troops to decapitate him what was that all about?
What offence has this son of the Xhosa nation committed for you to butcher him like an animal?
Why did you say he who will bring you this fighter's ears will be rewarded with beer?
Yooo! Queen Victoria, you put your trust in this hoodlum of yours.

Translated from the Sesotho original – Lefu La Morena Hintsha Ka 1835 – *by Goodenough Mashego*

NTATE SOBUKWE
Tsela Jeffrey Moloi
(Sesotho)

Jo, kakapa ya ma-Aforika
Wa makatsa Mangaliso
Graaff-Reneit torotswana ya Karoo
Wa re tswalla senatla ra leboha.

Le ha o hotse ka thata sebata
Empa o ne o bone bohlokwa ba thuto
Buka o ne o e phetle wa e phetlisisa
E neng e o bule kelello mme wa nama

Ba mphato wa hao ba o tseba, ha ba utlwe ka bo ba re.
Sekgowa o ne o se ntsha ka dinko
O ne o phatsitswe ka bohlale
O dula o le pele dithutong tsa hao

Bo sekolo sa Healdtown se ka o paka
Le yona yunivesiti ya Fort Hare
O ne o sa je dibuka feela
O ne o ja le yona politiki

O ile wa ikopanya le mekgatlo ya batjha
Wa ja dipolotiki tsa Bo- Aforika (Africanism)
Ba ka o paka le bona bo-Mda le bo-Lembede
O ba eteletse pele tseleng ya Bo-Aforika

O ne o bolele wa re Aforika e be ya Ma-Aforika
Mobu o be wa Ma-Aforika
Ma-Aforika a iketelle pele
Hobane bohloko bo utlwa ke bona

E ne e le ka selemo 1959
Moo o ileng wa kgena mme wa bopa mokgatlo wa PAC
Wa re Ma-Aforika tsohang le iketelle pele
Le iketelle pele jwaloka Ma-Aforika.

E ne e le ka selemo sa 1960
Moo o ileng wa re ho lekane ka di-dompas
Sena se ile sa kgentsha puso ya kgethollo
Mme e ile ya thunya ya fenetha Ma-Aforika

Mmuso wa kgethollo o ile wa o akgela tjhankaneng
Mme tjhankaneng wa dula dilemo-lemo
Kemoo Ma-Aforika a boneng bokgopo ba maburu
Le hore dipuisano tsona ha di thuse.

Eare e se khale
Puso ya kgethollo ya o akgela tjhankaneng hape
Wa ilo kwallwa sehleke-hlekeng sa Robben Island
Moo o ileng wa kwallwa o le mong jwaloka phoofolo.

Schleke-hlekeng wa ba mong
jwaloka phoofolo ya naha
Ho ne ho se motho eo o neng o bua le yena
O ne o kampa wa buisana le mobu wa sehleke-hleke
Utlwang sehloho sa puso ya kgethollo banna!

E ne e sa batle hore o kopane le batho ba bang
Kapa hona hore o dumediswe
Hothwe o tla kenya batho dipolotiki tse fosahetseng

O tla ba kenya le moya wa diabolose
O ile wa phela o le mong dilemo-lemo
Ha o kaba wa feela matla sebata sa MoAforika
Hobane o ne o tseba hore o lwanela lefatshe la Aforika
O ne o re: "Ha e khutle Aforika ya bo rona"

Ka mora dilemo tse robedi
Puso ya kgethollo ya re "o rata o sa rate, o utlwile"
Ya o lahlela hole toropong ya Kimberly
Moo moya wa hao o ileng wa fella teng.

Robala ka kgotso kakapa ya Mo-Aforika
Re tla dula re ntse re o hopola ho ya ho ile.
Lefatshe le ile ha le so khutle,
Robala ka kgotso kakapa ya Mo-Aforika!

FATHER SOBUKWE
Tsela Jeffrey Moloi

Praise, an African giant
Mangaliso you are amazing
A small town of Graaff-Reinet in the Karoo
We thank you for birthing us a giant

Though you grew up in trying situations
You still saw the value of education
A book you perused and re-read
That opened your mind and you spread

Your peers know you well they don't learn from the grapevine
Your nasal English was impeccable
You were blessed with wisdom
Always ahead in your education

Healdtown can bear testimony
Even the university of Fort Hare
You were not only into academics
You also dabbled in politics

You joined youth organisations
Indulged in the politics of Africanism
Lembede and Mda can testify for you
You led them on the path to Africanism

You would say Africa should be for Africans
The land shall belong to Africans
Africans should lead the continent

Because they are the ones feeling the pain
It was in 1959
When you split and formed the PAC
And said Africa should wake up and lead itself
Lead yourself like Africans

It was in 1960
When you rejected the Pass Laws
That angered the apartheid government
It shot and tortured Africans

The apartheid government threw you in jail
You spent years in incarceration
That's where you experienced the cruelty of the Boers
And that negotiations are not helpful

Not long afterwards
The apartheid government threw you in prison again
They locked you up at Robben Island
Where like an animal you were caged alone

On the island you were isolated like an animal
Without anybody to talk to
You'd rather talk to the soil of the island
Can you imagine such cruelty by the apartheid regime!

It didn't want you to meet other people
It even denied you mere greetings
They said you will incite wrong politics into people

And fill them with the spirit of the Devil

For years you lived alone
You didn't lose hope Lion of Africa
Because you knew you were fighting for the land of Africa
You were saying: "Mayibuye iAfrika."

After eight years
The apartheid government said you have finally repented
It banished you to the town of Kimberly
Where the ancestors finally summoned you

Rest in peace African giant
We'll always remember you
The land has still not yet returned
Rest in peace African giant!

Translated from the Sesotho original – Ntate Sobukwe – *by Goodenough Mashego*

SS MENDI
Tsela Jeffrey Moloi
(Sesotho)

E ne e le 21 Hlakola selemong sa 1917
Jonna koduwa ya wela Aforika Borwa
Sekepe sa SS Mendi sa tebetswa ka sehloho banna!
Bana ba thari-e-ntsho ba shwa ka sehloho!

Jonna, le lona le ne le ya kae le batlang?
Le ka ya ntweng jwang le sa tshwara dibetsa?
Le ne le rongwe ke mang ntweng ena?
Le ne le tjha le tshola eng?

Manyesemane a ne a le roma ka dife?
Ho baneng a ne a sa itwanele?
A ne a batla ho itshireletsa ka lona kgahlano le majeremane
Le ne le tla fumanang ntweng ena?

Jo, manyesemane a tla a le etsa diphoqo
Keng ya ho loka eo a kileng a le etsetsang yona?
A ne a le jelle naha a ba a le rekisa
Kajeno a batla le a lwanele.

Bana ba Rantsho le tla lwana jwang ka matsoho?
Le tla a etsang majeremane a dithunya-thunya?
Ho majeremane le ne le le ditshwene feela
A ne a tla reng ho bona ditshwene ka dithunya?

Bonang sehloho sa majeremane
SS *Darra* ya tla e totobetse ho SS *Mendi*
Ya pshwatla ya fenetha bana ba thari-e-ntsho
Bana ba thari-e-ntsho ba timela maqhobung a lewatle.

Ka lehlohonolo ba sala ba bang ba bana ba habo lona
Ba neng ba bina ba rapela
Le shwele le se merabe bana ba thari e-ntsho
Empa le shwele le le ngatana nngwe.

Jonna, bana ba thari-e-entsho
Le ha le lekile ho lwana dintwa tsa baditjhaba
Ke mang a le hlomphileng?
O na ma-Fora a kile a le hlompha?

Le ne le dula dikampong tsa o na jwaleka makgoba
Bana ba thari-e-ntsho ba pateloa thoko ba kgeloswa
Hobaneng le ne le sa patwe jwaloka ba bang?
E ne e le yona teboho ya bo-radikolone.

Le hona mona Aforika Borwa ke mang a ileng a le kgathalla?
Ke mang a neng a kgathalla hore le shwetse ntweng ya baditjhaba?
Le ne le ilo batla eng ntweng ya bo-dikolone le lona?
E ne e se hona ho "phapha" ha bana ba-Rantsho?

Kajeno nnete ha e tsebahale ho ditloholo tsa lona
Le ba kae bana ba thari-e-ntsho le shweletseng ntweng ena
Ekabe le ne le le dikete tse kae ho shwella balitjhaba?
A kae masapo le meya ya lona ditloholo lia pate?

Jonna, wena morena George V

O lebohile fela ka molomo
Mmuso wa kgethollo wa leboha masole a ona hwa utlwahala.
Empa bana ba thari-e-ntsho ba sala ba ahlame!

Ba bang ba lona le ne le le ba madi a borena
E kae naha le tjhelete ya teboho?
Jo, la tla la ba sehloho lona mayesemane le maburu?
Le re rona ditloholo tsa dikakapa tsena re le lebale jwang?

Jo bana ba morena George
Le tla patala neng sehloho seo le neng le se etse
Ka lefatshe le tjhelete eo le neng le e kwetele
Mohlomong le tla fodisa maqheba ao a ditloholo.

SS MENDI
Tsela Jeffrey Moloi

It was on 21 March 1917
Yooo, a tragedy befell South Africa
SS Mendi was ruthlessly sunken!
Africa's children died painful deaths!

Yooo, where were you going and what were you looking for?
How can you go to war unarmed?
Who sent you to that war?
Why were you burning and birthing?

Why did the English send you?
Why didn't they fight their own war?
Out of you they wanted to make human shields against the Germans
What did you stand to benefit from this war?

Yooo, the English made a mockery of you
What good have they ever done you?
They took your land and betrayed you
Today they want you to fight their war

How will you fight with your hands?
With what will you confront heavily armed Germans
Mere baboons you were to the Germans
What shall they do seeing baboons armed with guns?

See the cruelty of the Germans
SS *Darra* came and sunk SS *Mendi*

It broke down and killed Africa's children
Children of the soil got swallowed by a raging sea

Through sheer luck some survived the drowning
Those who were singing and dancing
You died separately children of the soil
But you died as a unit

Yoooo! Children of the soil
Though you tried to fight the wars of others
Who has ever honoured you?
Did the French ever respect you?

You were held like slaves in their camps
Children of the soil patted and misled
Why were you not treated like the rest?
Ill-treatment was the 'thank you' you received from colonisers

Even here in South Africa who has ever shown concern about you
Who has ever bothered that you died in a foreign war?
What were you doing fighting a coloniser's war?
Weren't you just being forward like all children of the soil?

To your grandchildren the truth remains a mystery to this day
How many black people died in this war
How many thousands of you died in this war?

Where lie your bones and your spirits for your grandchildren to bury?
Yooo! King George V
You only verbally said "thank you"
The apartheid government showed real gratitude to its soldiers
Children of the soil were left poor!

Some of you were of royal blood
Where is land and money to reward you?
How cruel can the English and the Boers be?
How do you expect us to forget how you treated us?

Yooo! Children of George
When are you going to pay reparations
With land and money you robbed us
Maybe you might start healing the wounds of our grandchildren.

Translated from the Sesotho original – SS Mendi – *by Goodenough Mashego*

GENETIC LOTTERY
Nedine Moonsamy

The doctor asked
If there is a history of cancer
In your family.

Your parents,
flanking you
like solemn bookends,
say,
No.

Later,
your mother
your father
both
whisper
private confessions
that your paternal uncle,
that your maternal great-granny
had cancer.

Weighing their guilt,
they seek absolution
for this genetic lottery,
where they had bought the ticket,
but you had lost on the gamble.

E HLAGILE
Mapule Ramaila Moswane
(Sepedi)

E hlagile ya boMahlagaume mmina phoofolo tsoko ya mmala tsoko.
Sehlaga sa mašianoke se tšerwe e a tšutšutla go hlakahlakane.
Mehlare e a tlheretlhephelwa e hlobaela ka phefo.
E hlagetše bašemanyana ba moremohlabana.
E hlagetše bana ba balata le ba bahlanka.
Ba tšwa kgole le kgauswi ba hlaganetše go ba masogana.
Bangwe ba tšwa kgauswi ka Mahlakole.
Bangwe ba tšwa kgole Sehlakwane
Bangwe ba tšwa kgolekgole Mamehlake.
Ba tšwele mahlalagading ba na le mahlajana.
Bohle ba phafogile ga go yo a hlohlonwago ke boroko.
Lehono ke lehono mahlasedi a letšatši a ba hlabetše.
Mahlo a ditšhaba ka moka a lebile go bona.
Re re mahlogonolo go bona tseleng ya bona
Ya go yo hlahlelelwa go ba masogana.
Tsela ke e tee ga go yo a hlahlathago ba lebile gona.
Mphatong ba lebile ka Sehlabeng.
Ka dipelong ba re hlakoleng go a sepelwa.
Tseleng ba fetile Mmathobehlale ka go la mpogošo.
Ba phatšitše Mmamabu a mmatšitlana
Ya tšitla motho dinyaraga tša re tšitlaa!
Meetse ba feta ba enwa Mohlakaneng.
Go fihla ba fihlile mphatong wa mahlalerwa.
Go bona ke gae ga mahlaku bjale.
Ka bohlabela ba hlapeditše ka Mahlwakgomo.
Ka leboa ba ukametše Mohlakaneng.
Sa kua kgojana ba bona Sehlale ka mahlo.

Mašemong go bonala mahlaka ao a se go a omela sa ruri.
Ditlhaka di sa tšwa go phalala mogwang o buletšwe.
Sa kgauswana ba bona Lehlajaneng.
Le ge e šetše e hlagile, dihlagele di sa hlagela.
Sejo e tlile go ba mohlatlo wo o hlatlotšwego ke dikgarebe
Ka lapeng la yo mogolo ka kgati kgorong.
Dihlamukelamaledu ke barutiši ba sekolo seo.
Dithuto ke tša gore mohlako o a hlalefiša,
Ka ge e le bomahlwaadibona.
Dikgalabje le tšona di fela di šebetša ka la botšofadi
Ka ge a maswa mahlaku a ema ka a matala.
Le ge difahlego di laetša go hlagala ba sa e hlatlegela ya loya.
Ba bangwe baditšana ba tshetše le Sehlale.
Ka magae basadi ga ba sa tseba le go hlamula.
Megopolo e hlahlametše e a hlahlatha.
Ge ba gopola gore mala a bona a gokae ka seo sebaka.
Mphato ke wa Dihlagahlagane dinonyana tša go aga dihlaga.
E tla fihla nako ya go aloga hlathing.
Moo o tla go kwa mongwe a itheta a re:
Ke nna Maahlagane a bo tlhahlamedupi nonyana ya go bitša pula.
A re hee lena dikgarebe ke lena le sa nthetego,
Ke tla retwa ke kgaetšedi'aka Mahlako a Hlabirwa le Hlapogadi
A ntheta a ntheteletša bothakga.
A re kwaa kgaetšedi' aka Hlware ya go ja dipotšanyane
O tšo tšea selo se sethata bonna thabeng!

IT HAS HAPPENED
Mapule Ramaila Moswane

It happened in the home of Mahlagaume whose totem is a certain animal
The nest of a hamerkop has been stolen it's stormy it's confusion
Trees shake wildly threatened by a strong wind
It happened to young boys
It happened to children of servants and subjects
They come from far and wide rushing to be young men
Some come nearer to Mahlakole
Some come further at Sehlakwane
Some from far away at Mamehlake
They emerged wiser out of adolescence
They are all alert none is sleepy
Today's the day the sun shines on them
A million eyes watch them carefully
We wish them well on their journey
To be initiated into manhood
There's only one road no one goes astray they are all headed there
Their school is in Sehlabeng
In their hearts they say we'll see what happens
They passed Mmathobehlale on their left
They also walked past Mmamabu the grinder
Which grinds a person until his back thighs are mush!
They stop to drink their water at Mohlakaneng
They have arrived at the school of the wolves
It is their new home now
On the east they are guarded by Mahlwakgomo
On the south they look down at Mohlakaneng
Further down they see Sehlale

In the field they see canes not yet dry
Ditlhaka di sa tšwa go phalala mogwang o buletšwe.
They see Lehlajaneng nearer to them.
Even after it has started, nests are still nesting
Their food shall have been prepared by young women
In the home of the elder it's stick fighting
Bearded men are teachers at this school
The lessons are that poverty makes one wiser
Because they are experienced
Old men also throw in their two cents' worth
For the young should learn more from the old
Though their faces look old they still have wisdom
Some impoverished people crossed Sehlale
At home women cannot even speak
Their minds are restless they wander
When they think about where their children are at this moment
Initiation school is for Dihlagahlagane birds that build their nests
Time for graduation will come
Where you'll hear self-praise like
I am Maahlagane of tlhahlamedupi, the rain bird
Saying you women are the ones not praising me
I will be praised by my sister Mahlako of Hlabirwa of Hlapogadi
Praising me for my artfulness
Saying listen to my brother a Python that swallows goats
He has brought manhood from the mountain

Translated from the Sepedi original – E Hlagile – *by Goodenough Mashego*

BHAQ' OLUNGAMUNWE
Aphiwe Masibonge Namba
(Zulu)

Nina bakaSenzagakhona
Nina zindlondlo ezinkulu
Ngoba beqonde ukumdingisa uZulu
Ashabalala amaqhinga ongxiwankulu

Ngiyomemeza kufinyelele eNyakatho,
eNingizimu, Mpumalanga naseNtshonalanga
Abasiki bebunda bayakhuluma

bathi masibhong emswaneni

Jama! Sixolele Jama, ngobuwula nathi savuma
Ikhambi lisekhona bantu bakithi ningadangali

Ngofakaza kuzwe bonke namahlongandlebe:
nazi ezinohlonze enginiphatelezona,

Cikic' imbici ubhekisise,
vul amehlo uhlolisise

Kungani usuzikhohliwe?
Kungani engasithi usucheme ngabezizwe
waze wakhishw inyumbazana esihlalweni sakho
sobukhosi?

Uyinkosi, singamakhosi

LIGHT THAT CANNOT BE COMPARED
Aphiwe Masibonge Namba

You of Senzangakhona
You great, big black mambas
Because they aimed to exile Zulu.
Then the schemes disappeared from the authorities

I shall shout until I am heard in the North,
In the South, East, and West
The news collectors are talking

They say we have to accept the inevitable

Jama! Forgive us Jama, because of foolishness we also agreed.
The solution still exists don't give up.
I shall witness until all mischievous people hear:
Here is interesting news that I have come to share with you.

Wipe your eyes clean and look carefully,
Open your eyes and analyse properly

Why have you forgotten?
Why do you look as if you have sided with foreigners
you have even been marginalised from your seat of power?

You are a king, we are kings

Translated from the Zulu original – Bhaq' Olungamunwe – *by Innocentia Mhlambi*

CAMAGU
Kwazi Ndlangisa
(Zulu)

Ngiwukukhanya ezweni labansundu,
Ngixosha ubumnyama bungekazalwa kuhle bonyenzi
ebusweni bomhlaba/
Ngingowenzalo ezweni laseAfrika
Ufakazi, bheka ubudlelwano besikhumba sami nelanga
Ngazalwa ngowesifazane njengakho konke okuhamba
phezu kwalomhlaba
Amandla ngawembeswa ngookhokho nookhokhokazi
endulo mina ngingekazalwa nangomcabango
Ngimdala kunami
Ngimncane ezweni
Kwamoya kukhulwa ezweni lamathongo,
Ungibona nje angibazi ubuthongo bakwaMhlaba
Ngithwele izintaba namagquma ezizukulwana zakwaNtu,
amaphupho nezifiso ezafel' emafini zicinga ukukhanya
kwelanga
Zazihamba nokukhanya zingazelele
Lokhu kuyangibulala
Hleze futhi khona lokhu kuyangiphilisa
Pho ke mina bengiyini ngingabanga wuhlanya,
Nakhu ngibhadula lapho livuka nanxa lidonsa izikhumba
ilanga
Yimi lowo ngilandela amaloba wezithunywa zikaMenzi
ehlane nasemkhathini
Inhloso ukuthola izimpendulo zayizolo ukuze
ngikhanyisele inamuhla
Ngesiqubulo sika Makukhanye, sithokoze isizwe
sakwaMoya.
Camagu!

CAMAGU
Kwazi Ndlangisa

I am the light in the land of brown people,
I chase away darkness before it is birthed just like the morning star on the face of the earth
I am a descendant of Afrika
Evidence, look at the relationship of my skin and the sun
I was born of a woman just like everything on the face of the earth
My powers were given to me by my ancestors long ago before I was conceived as thought
I am older than myself
I am the youngest in the world
Just like wind one grows up in the world of the ancestors
As you see me I do not know the sleep of the Earth
I am carrying mountains and hills of the generations of Humanity,
Dreams and aspirations that died in the clouds looking for light
They travelled with light unawares
That this is killing me
Perhaps this too also gives me life
So how can it be that I am not mad,
Here I am walking aimlessly when the sun rises and sets
Here I am following the writings of the messengers of the Creator in the fields and forests
The aim is to get answers of yesterday so that I shine the light for today
All hailing Makukhanye, the nation of Moya is pleased.
Camagu!

Translated from the Zulu original – **Camagu** *– by Innocentia Mhlambi*

IZOLO-KUSASA
Kwazi Ndlangisa
(Zulu)

hohee! hamba minyaka...
wacathula ngempela nezithunzi zethu wayosithela
usibona nje sihamba sihlanganisa izingcezu zakho
ezindongeni zemicabango
sesibambelele kwesakuncela kuCosi,
efika nesithombe sikaGogo, nathi belu sizukulwana sakhe
sizungeze umlilo
izinganekwane zisithatha zisibeka ezweni
lakwaMhlabamumbe
lapho kusala umzimba ngelithi emafini kusekhaya likamoya
esiphelezela ngemilolozelo nxashana sithatha inyathuko
ebheke kwam'fuziselo wokufa

loluchungechunge ke oluhlobe ngolwazi nobunyonicu
lugijima egazini kulemithambo
isizukulwana sakwaNtu sikreza kwegwanse ngezaqheqhe
silokhu sihogela umkhondo womlando
siqobola amagquma namathafa
sibheke kwingomuso elingenazithembiso
ngethemba lokuba siyoyibona phambili indlela

yingakho ke esebeyihambile lendlela
bebeshumayela phezu kwelithi, "Mazibuye Emasisweni"
nokho nathi belu sibone kukuhle sidle ngalo oludala
ukhezo
ngethemba lokuba okwaphilisa okhokho nokhokhokazi,
nathi kuyosiphilisa
nangazo lezi zikhathi ekuthiwa ezokugcina sisabhadula
kuyo indlela enameva

kwaphika ingebhe, yathi nxa singazivikela ngezimbadada
izizukulwana ziyowacinga ziwathole kweziphi izinkalo
amaloba wethu?

lenyathuko eyayizolo injalo nje ingeyanamuhla
lenyathuko eyamandulo injalo nje ingeyaphakade
lenyathuko eyami nawe, lenyathuko eyama-Afrika
nxa ufuna ukuyithatha, ungalibali ukwebuza lesosikhumba
yebo sona sihle, sinjalo nje siyakhazimula
yingakho size sixhophe nawe uqobo
lapho sowubona luvindi,
ubozicinga kwisibuko sakho, inhlabathi
hleze kwembuleke ulwembu uzikhumbule
nangomuso kusawusuku, usangayibona ebheke ekhaya
kini, kuwe
hleze lokhu okucinga kulamagumbi amathathu omhlaba
kwakuthola ungekalahleki nakwelokuqala

YESTERDAY-TOMORROW
Kwazi Ndlangisa

hohee! … time flies
you walked by slowly with our shadows and disappeared
as you see us now we walk piecing together your pieces
in the walls of the minds
holding on to what we learnt from Cosi
who came with Grandma's photo, and we too her
generation, sat around the fire
folktales taking us to places like the land of a certain World
where the body remains saying the clouds is the home of
the soul
accompanying us with lullabies when we talk a journey
towards the place like death

this long knowledge adorned with expertise runs in the
blood of these very veins
the generation of Humanity draw milk directly from the
udder full of fresh cream
we are always following the trail of history
we go up the hills and fields
we are looking to a tomorrow without promises
hoping that we shall see the path along the way

that is why those who have travelled the path
preached it loudly that, "Let us return to our traditions"
we also saw it fit that we should eat from the spoons of the
past
with the trust that what made our ancestors live will also
make us live
even during these days that are said to be the end of times

we still walk on this prickly path
fear defied, saying we need to protect ourselves with sandals
our generations, where will they search and find our writings?

this path is from yesterday and even so of today
this path is from the past and even so of eternity
this path is mine and yours, this path is for Africans
if you want to take it, don't forget to shed your old skin
yes it is a beautiful skin, and it is a shiny one
that is why it also blinds you
and you no longer see clearly
you must search for your reflection in your mirror, the soil
maybe the cobweb in your eyes will be removed and you remember yourself
tomorrow is still a day, you will still see your path home, in you
maybe what you search for in these three corners of the earth found you before you got lost in the first one

Translated from the Zulu original – Izolo-Kusasa *– by Innocentia Mhlambi*

EKHAYA KUTHULE
Mawushe Selby Nomnganga
(Xhosa)

Abantu abanoxolo bathule,
Kanti sithi abo.

Isijwili esingaka,
Kuthulwe kangaka.

Inene Anene[1] konakele,
Nabanye benziwa njengawe,
Balityalwa kwathula kwathi tu.

Ekhaya kuthule kuthe tu,
Inene Uyi-uyi[2] konakele.

Sothuka omel' emqaleni
Kufungwe ngobulungisa,
Obuza kulungisa.

Cwaka akuviwa nelimdaka
Kuthula ekhaya kuthi tu!

---

1 Anene Booysen was brutally disembowelled after being raped and left to die in Bredasdorp, Western Cape province in 2013. She was found alive but later succumbed to her injuries.
2 Uyinene Uyi-uyi Mrhwetyana was raped and hit over the head with a weight scale by an employee with a criminal record at the South African Post Office when she went to collect a parcel. She was buried in a shallow grave in the criminal's backyard.

IT IS QUIET AT HOME
Mawushe Selby Nomnganga

People who are peaceful are quiet
And that is us

Such quietness
So much silence

Indeed Anene things are bad
Even others were done the same as you
They were forgotten and it was quiet

At home it is quiet
Indeed Uyi-uyi things are bad

we were shocked till our throats
justice was sworn
to fix things

so quiet not even a word from the blacks
At home it is quiet

Translated from the Xhosa original – **Ekhaya Kuthule** – *by Innocentia Mhlambi*

ZAPHEL' IIMBOKODO
Azile Ntloni
(Xhosa)

Ndibolekeni usiba nephepha ndibhale.
Ndiphalaze imbilini yam ngalomzuzu,
Ndigragramle ndibhodle ngelixesha.
Ndibelutshaba nexhoba kuni

Ibizwa ngantoni lento yenzekayo?
Manyala mani lana alapha eMzantsi?
Baphel' abafazi ngenxa yenkohlakalo yamadoda,
Zaphel' iintombi ngenxa yenu!

Kwabangasa iimbokodo zigengeleze phantsi!!
Kwabangasa iinkedama ziyanda, zidinga oomama.
Ndithi ndakuma entabeni ndive ilizwi lenkazana ikhala,
Icela uxolo kuba utata efuna ukuva imbewu yakhe.

Ndithi ndisamamele apho ndive umfazi esitsho
esikaNandi.
Ezicelela uxolo kuba ebon' ukufa kufikile,
Konakelephi na madoda kulungiswe?
Senze ntoni lena esingeke saxolelwa ngayo?

Siphi isazela nosizi kulento nisenza yona?
Sitye ntoni kabani ebekungafanelanga siyitye?
Siphenduke amaxhoba kubafowethu mvanje.
Baphenduk' izilwane, namabhubesi angasiqweng nanini.

Asazi nongakwazi ukusikhusela ubonanje,
Oh Mvelingqangi ngenelela, Mncedi wenkedama!
Iintliziyo zethu zinxkunguphele asikwazi kuxola.

Eyehlula amadoda idluliselwa ebafazini.
Hayibo yenziwa njani lonto!!
Ipheph' endibhala kulo limanzi ziinyembezi.
Ngeba ndiyaqhubeka ndibhale,
Ntonje ndiphelelwe yindawo yokubhala.

WOMEN ARE BEING FINISHED
Azile Ntloni

Lend me a pen and paper to write
So I can get this pain off my chest
I want to roar in this minute
Let me be an enemy and victim to you

What do you call this?
What curse is here in South Africa?
Women are being finished because of men's cruelty
Girls are dying because of you!

At dawn a woman lies dead!
At dawn orphans increase needing mothers
When I stand on top of a mountain I hear a woman's cry
Crying for forgiveness because the father wants to feel his seed

While still listening I hear a woman crying
Asking for forgiveness seeing that death has come
What has happened men?
What is it that thing that we will not be forgiven for?

Where is the conscience and sympathy in what you are doing to us?
Whose food did we eat that we were not supposed to eat?
We have become victims to our brothers
They have become beasts that can devour you anytime

We do not know how to protect ourselves
Lord intervene, helper of orphans

Our hearts are in pain we can't even be in peace
What has defeated is passed on to women

Why would you do that?!
The paper that I am writing on is wet with tears
I would continue to write
The thing is that I have run out of space to write on.

Translated from the Xhosa original – Zaphel' Iimbokodo – *by Innocentia Mhlambi*

KWANELE
Sihle Ntuli
(Zulu)

Bafwethu, kanti samadoda anjani
okwaqala ngezingoma zoBaba:
sizwa kodwa singezwa
kwi ihlazo elibi
elinganamhloni!
laze laculwa
laduma kumsakazo kukalisa kweZulu.
sakhala isiginci savala umsindo,
zashawa izandla zabekwa kuMa.
ungambiza kanjani
umuntu omthandayo
nge thambo lami lekentaki?
uwazi kamhlophe ukuthi lona lelothambo
amazinyo alenza njani.
akukukho thando
amazinyo esedabula
akukho thando
izinyo eliqonda nqo kwithambo
akukho thando
ithambo amazinyo eselihlafuna
akukho thando
uma selipheleli ithambo liyimvuthu
kungani madoda nishiya izimvuthu!

Bafwethu kanti samadoda anjani?
ilanga kudala lashona kwizindlela zakudala
ubudoda abusavezwa ngesandla esiqinile,
indoda eqotho uyibona ngezenzo zayo
iphinde futhi ithambe iboniswe, ilalele

ayiwaphindi amaphutha obaba nomkhulu
ilanga lokuhlonipheka livuka ngayo lendoda
ukugqama kwayo kufundise abanye
befise ukuba nesithunzi sayo.

Bafwethu kanti samadoda anjani?
baningi abesifazane abazi abanye abahlukunyezwa
kodwa phakathi kwethi abesilisa
kwenziwa yini amehlo avese avaleka
sijike zimphumphumthi
abadlwenguli singababoni behleli maduze nathi

Bafwethu kanti samadoda anjani?
kumele kube njani?
madoda asideli?
kambe kuyaphefumleka isizwe liyimifula yezinyembezi?
silala sizwa ngezintombi ziyalahleka zingatholakali
sivuka sekumemezwa!
ukuthi zitholakele umphefumulo wazo ungaseko
umuntu angaze ezitshela
ukuthi uphupha kabi
kanti uphila saka!
lonakala ilizwe lethu
selibolile!
shwele modada sekwanele!

IT IS ENOUGH
Sihle Ntuli

My brothers, what kind of men are we
what started with the songs of our Fathers:
we are hearing but we do not listen
it is a bad shame
shameless!
it is even sung about
made known in the radio Zulu.
the guitar played and covered up the noise,
hands clapped and we placed upon Ma.
how can you call
someone you love
you Kentucky bone?
when you know very well that bone
suffers under teeth.
that is not love
when teeth tear it up
there is no love
where tooth goes straight to the bone
there is no love
when the bone is chewed up
there is no love
when the bone has been chewed up into pieces
why men would you leave behind pieces!

My brothers, what kind of men are we?
the sun long set upon the ways of old
manhood is no longer exhibited by strong hands,
an honourable man is seen by his acts
again he is soft to being advised and listens

he does not repeat the mistakes of our ancestors
the sun of respectability makes this man rise up
his brilliance teaches others
and they also wish to have his dignity.

My brothers, what kind of men are we?
so many women know of others who have been abused
but within us men
what makes our eyes to shut close
and turn to be blind
rapists we do not see yet they are seated among us

My brothers, what kind of men are we?
how must we be?
men can't we get enough?
are you able to breath when the nation is just rivers of tears?
every night we go to bed hearing about missing girls
we wake up when there are shouts!
that they have been found when their breath has departed
one might even fool himself
that it is a nightmare
yet he is alive!
our land has been despoiled
it has decayed!
Pardon, men it is enough!

Translated from the Zulu original – **Kwanele** – *by Innocentia Mhlambi*

MONNA KE NKU
Mosimo Kagiso Phakane
(Sepedi)

Monna ke nku o llela teng
Koša go tšwa kutung ya dipelo tša banna ba diatla tša go kgamathela madi
Marapo a thuthumela nke bjang ge bo bona sesasedi
Ba tuntetša mahloko gare ga tša go galaka
Tša bona dintho di garoša namana tša mmele
Ao hle mošemanyana aka
A go hlokagale go fihla dillo le mahloko
Gare ga leswiswi la bošegogare bja marega
Ešita le bagale ba na le mafokodi
Ke go adima tšaka ditsebe
Ge lefase le thiba tša lona ka šupa-baloi
Ge o ikwa nke go ledimo le legolo la bogale ka gare ga gago
Ke go adima sefuba saka
Go nyorelela meetsefula ao a imelago mahlo a gago
Bohloko ke mpholo
Bo dumelle go ela o tla humana khomotšo
Ke go nea yaka pelo
Go go gopotša gore lerato le a go tshwanela
Le kakatlele ka tše pedi diatla
O eme o keteke nke lesea ge le bona mmago lona
O se swabišwe ke go kgangwa ke lethabo
Ke go adima maswafo aka
Ge o ikwa nke o rwele dithaba ka dikgara
Nke o rwele bophara bja lefase ka magetla
Kholofelo le tshepho di go furaletše
Bophelo bo rata go ka go phonyoga
Lefase le go ntšheditše a diketepula
Ba kgauswi le ya gago pelo

Ba go hlapa diatla
Diatla tše tšaka ke gae
Ke tla go phumula megokgo ya lehono
Le mekgeledi ya maloba le maabane
Etshwa bohloko, o tla humana khutšo le khomotšo

MEN DON'T CRY
Mosimo Kagiso Phakane

Men don't cry
A song from the bottom of the hearts of men with bloodied hands
Bones shiver like grass when a whirlwind approaches
They drown their sorrows in spirits
Their wounds are heart-wrenching
Please my boy
There's no need to hide pain and tears
In the quietness of a winter night
Even brave men have weaknesses
As I listen to you
When the world refuses to listen to you
When you feel a raging wind of anger inside you
I lend you my chest
That flood of tears that weighs down your eyes
Pain is toxic
Let it flow you will find relief
Here is my heart
To remind you you deserve love too
Receive it with both hands
Arise and celebrate like an infant when it sees its mother
Find no shame in expressing happiness
Here are my lungs
When you feel the load is too heavy
As if the world rests on your shoulders
That hopes and faith have deserted you
That life is trying to slip off your hands
The world is out to ruin you
They are nearer to your heart

They deny knowing you
In my hands you will find home
I'll wipe away your tears today
And those of yesterday and the day before
Release your pain, you'll find peace and comfort

Translated from the Sepedi original – Monna Ke Nku *– by Goodenough Mashego*

SELLO SA MOSADI
Mosimo Kagiso Phakane
(Sepedi)

Le ba botše bagolo ba rena le re
Re dutše magala ka marago
Re pipile dintho tša go šiiša ka diaparo
Tšela re bego re di holofetše diatla
Di tletše meetlwa ya moretšhe
Di kgamathetše madi

Le ba botšiše borakgolo le re
Ba ba tlogeletše dife dithuto boKgethi le boMašilo
Ba itirile mašilo a go lahlwa
Thari ya maabane ga e sa bolokegile
Ba thubagantšha le metšega ya meetse a go hlweka
Gae ga go sa le gae, ga go borutho go a šiiša

Le ba botšiše bokoko le re
Ke gona ge ba re bogadi ke lebitla na
Re tsena ka a mabedi,
Ra felesetšwa ka sefela, re rwelwe ke diphiri
Ke gona ge ba re monna ke selepe na
O a rema a remelela le ba go tswalwa ke yena
Ga di kgotlellege, ke dipshešamare

Le ba botšiše babolai ba rena le re
Tša bona dipelo ba di lahlile kae
Kwelobohloko yona e ile kae
Ba tlo re khutšiša ge go fetile ba ba kae
Re tla iphihla kae ra go bitša gae
Khutšo yona re tlo e humana kae

Le ba botše bagologolo le re
Tša rena ditopo di ka se hlobogwe
Le go bolokwa di ka se bolokwe
Khutšo yona, re ka se e bone
Di fetile le meetse le matlakala
Di fihlilwe moragorago ga dithaba

THE CRY OF A WOMAN
Mosimo Kagiso Phakane

Tell our elders that
We are not comfortable here
We hide ugly wounds behind robes
That which we hoped for
Are full of thorns and thistles
They are dripping blood

Ask our forefathers
What lessons did Kgethi and Mašilo leave us
They have become lazy throw-aways
Yesterday's generation is no longer safe
They even destroy jars where clean water is stored
Home is no longer warm, it's hurting

Ask our grandmothers if
This is what they mean that divorce is alien
We walk in eyes wide open
Accompanied in hymns, carrying secrets
Is this what they mean that man is an axe
He chops even his own children
This is intolerable, it's despicable

Ask our murderers
Where did their hearts die
What happened to their mercy
How many should die before we rest
Where shall we hide to call it home
Where will we find peace

Tell our ancestors
Our corpses will never be mourned
They won't even be buried
We will know no peace
It is gone with the wind
They are hidden behind mountains

Translated from the Sepedi original – Sello Sa Mosadi – *by Goodenough Mashego*

ISIKHALO SOMFAZI OMNYAMA!
Yvonne Busisiwe Phyllis
(Xhosa)

Ndibuyisele emhlabeni mbumbi wam
Kakade esona sigqibo
Siphakathi kokufa nokuphila
Kwanokuphila ikwakuko ukufa
Ndenze ndibe mnye nomhlaba

Xa ndilele, ndiphumle
Xa ndihleli ndiyalwa
Amadabi am awanasiphelo
Xa ingelulo ucalucalulo
Yimfazwe ebufazini bam
Ndenze ndibe mnye nomhlaba

Xa ingeyiyo indlala ne ntsokolo, lityala
Ndinqwenela umhlaba, kodwa andinalo ithemba
Umhlaba ngo wabantu abamhlophe?
Abamhlophe bayadakasa, umnt'omnyama uyakhasa
Inene ubunzima sibuthwele,
Ndenze ndibe mnye nomhlaba

Bayandibuza: "kanti liphi na ithemba"
Andinaz'impendulo,
Umqweno mnye,
Xa ndilele, makube cum
Ndide ndivuke eluxolweni
Ndide ndivuke enkululekweni

A BLACK WOMAN'S CRY!
Yvonne Busisiwe Phyllis

Return me to the earth my creator
That is the only decision
We are between death and living
Even living is still death in itself
Make me one with the earth

When asleep am at rest
When awake I am fighting
My battles are endless
If it is not discrimination
it is the war on my womanhood
Make me one with the earth

If it is not hunger and suffering, it is a case
I long for the land, but I do not have hope
Land is for white people?
White people are flying, while black people are crawling
We are suffering indeed
Make me one with earth

They ask me: "where is the hope"
I do not have the answers
I have one wish
When am asleep let it be quiet
Until I wake up peacefulness
Until I wake up in freedom

Translated from the Xhosa original – Isikhalo Somfazi Omnyama! – *by Innocentia Mhlambi*

I AM YOUR DAUGHTER
Tshifhiwa Itai Ratshiungo

i. i asked mma, if he were here to listen would he say, 'i am not your father'?

ii. at four, i carried a stuffed gorilla on my back the way a mother does her child. for a towel, i used a jersey. i did not have a song to lull this dead thing i imagined a crying baby. i imagined using the back of its tiny hand to rub sleep off its eyes. i rocked and rocked and hummed my baby to sleep. baba found and watched me like he saw a thing in me. it was not a proud smile on his face. after my name, he called me musadzi. [mylittleboy]-woman, [mylittleboy]-my daughter, "til his death.

iii. i want to say that i am still, even so softly, your son baba. in this dress, will he, mma? will he call me my name with a smile on his face the way he used to? or will he, like you, ask about the grandchildren you wish to have?

iv. i will adopt

but those are not your children

children are children

and you will have your own

i don't even want children mma

so that's why you love… boys?

v. because i keep myself beautiful, she thinks i love the mirror. because i sang at the mirror in her clothes, she thought of it a demon. because she called me a demon, she prayed without being a praying woman. she spewed tongues upon me, dressed beautifully – so much that she fears loving myself too much will end at loving men. and is that what i want? will it please me to bend my body for another man? she asked.

vi. i found a boy and he loves me like a house on fire. wholly. all insecurity in me burnt to ashes: that i feel myself a girl half the time, that i feel myself a girl most times, that i am a girl, that god gave me a body for both, that i am not gay mma. i am the way i am and there's no language for a name i can give you to call me. i don't feel taboo – the praying you now do is full of lies.

vii. how she prays is like i am the gorilla and she is me. rocking and rocking and the passion of her tongues wanting to revive the son she birthed. and she is crying because i am dead. and she is crying because there is a demon making me love the mirror. and she thinks of my body bent. and her prayer will not relent because she will lose me. like the way she did when she said i am not your mother. and that's why, baba, i asked her then if you will say it too. after i tell you who i am, will you want me back so much you pray me out of damnation? are you a prayer baba?

viii. i am not this way because i love to be. i am your daughter.

THE NATIVE CHOICE
Warren Jeremy Rourke

You place your hand over mine
at the Pretoriuskop Wimpy
in the Kruger National Park
and say
I'm loving Africa.
       I smile at Thabiso, our grumpy waitron,
and think of billionaire fellow South Africans,
the Emirates, and Nazo! Meals

You take your hand away
to scroll through the kill
at the side of the road
and say
I can't believe we saw this.
       I look around at the content visitors,
and think of captive-bred lion hunting,
trophies, and imports verses exports.

You reach out your hand
towards the place of my heart
to remind me that I'm not alone
and say
Come, let's go.
       I frown at the bill, the idea of gratuity,
and think of how I'm going to tell you,
Thabiso, and everyone else,
I'm Staying.

MY MOTHER'S HOUSE
Dimakatso Anthea Sedite

When you lose your mother to death, you spend your life looking for her,
amongst small stones, on corners of your dishcloth,
behind broken cars.
You fear throwing beans into a pot, lest she's there, hiding amongst them.

You carry your childhood everywhere: the comfort of overcooked food,
sugar on pumpkin pulp, oil in cabbage, doilies on the sofa.
You search for yourself all over: in books, in music, in corners of your nails.

I gaze at the sunset, hoping she will emerge, with her gait.
I feel her wide like an umbrella, try to clip her memory to my chest,
back to my childhood, back to the comfort of her food.

My knuckles crochet this din with the aid of mops and brooms.
Floors are shiny, bare, like peeled onion. Curtains bite their muteness
and the memory of people who are now plastic on walls.

Chairs are my four guests, a choir of owls sings carols on a TV screen.
An ant enters, looking for overcooked food,
next to knuckles of chairs, finding only fading religion.

ON THE PEOPLE'S POWER
Noluthando Mpho Sibisi

Always remember the intricacies of breathing:
The breadth of your lungs
The depth of your breath
The width of your breast
Now,
When the cavity between your neck and your stomach is
under threat of being crushed
Strangled by authority, starved by anxiety
Breathe,
widen your claim to life
deepen your uptake of air
broaden the vista of revolution
Whatever you do, do not forget to draw breath
In through your fleshy nose
And out of your full lips
From your grandmother's hands into your own;
you have inherited time
Intimate knowledge that rest is rebellion.

MALOHLE
(Go, Matete Motsoaledi)
Moses Seletiša
(Sepedi)

A mantšhi ga'rena, Malohle.
Ga e sa le meno re šinne
Dipounama di ngamotšwe wa mphaka go ilalo Mola le
diatla hlogong re fega re fegile
A gago mafotwana ke a bone maloba
A setla le ya moloi pelo
Ke nnete, Matete.
Nkgo ya babina tlhantlhagane e ribegilwe
Go lla go tla thušang?
Nama še le yona e latola letswai
Re hlahuna phure re hlokola
Mola tala re gata e bola
O re šiile tsatsanka ya leswene la Rakgwadi Dipelo ga di
dudišege Motebejane
Di sa tšwela pele di gerema le a bjaša mafata Wa hlogo
moro re o fokoditše
Mekgokgo e thenkgolloga makaleng a sefahlego
Re hutša go go bušetša popelong
Gore nke o leke bophelo ka leswa Malohle 'a Matlala
'a Motebejane Phorogohlo košeng ya 'go ruta bothaga
bothakga'
Ge e le peu o gašitše ka tša gago tša makgwakgwa
Re tla šala re lema joko e dutše 'phogong re e hlwa re go
belegi magetleng a kgopolo tša rena #RE BATHO LE
MMINO, MATABANE!

MALOHLE
(To Matete Motsoaledi)
Moses Seletiša

Words fail us, Malohle
Since our teeth gnashed
Our lips still sagging like a knife
Bewildered and puzzled we have been
I saw your kids the other day
I couldn't help but empathise
Indeed, Matete.
The calabash of those whose totem is a finch has bowed out
What good shall crying achieve?
It's not the same
We are walking on a rotting green
Your death was sudden and untimely
Our hearts can't find rest Motebejane
They still wander in search of peace
As for tears we have shed
Tears flowing down our faces
We wish to send you back to the womb
So you can try life afresh Malohle a Matlala a Motebejane
Phorogohlo in a song 'go ruta bothaga bothakga'
With your rough hands you planted beautiful seeds
We will till the land with a yoke on our shoulders carrying you on the shoulders of our thoughts #RE BATHO LE MMINO MATABANE!

Translated from the Sepedi original – **Malohle** *– by Goodenough Mashego*

UMZILI ONGAPHEZI
Siwaphiwe Fortune Shweni
(Xhosa)

Yimin'enkulu kwiintsapho ebe zinamakhwenkwe
asentabeni
Yimin'emnandi kwizidla nyama.
Yimin'emnandi kwizihlobo zikaDl'omdlayo
Yimin'emnandi kubahlobokazi bakaMabil'ebanda.
Yimin'emnandi nakwabo basuka entabeni.
Kumnandi kotoki, nditsho nakwihag'imbala kuba intsipho
zikhona
Kumnandi: kuyayiyizelwa, kubethw'ingqongqo
kuyangqungqwa, kuyombelwa
kuvuyiswana: neentsapho ebe zise abantwan'entabeni
kunye namakhwenkw'abuy'entabeni
Kukho umzali ongumama: okwathi ngaminazan'ithile
emva kokunikezela umntwana wakhe emadodeni
ukuze amenz'indoda abe yindoda kweli khaya.
Wath'esavul'ucango eqwabulul'iintong'emehlweni
wee-ntlaa! Ngengub'emhloph'emgc'ubomvu
ixhonyw'ethangweni
Kuloo mama imini yomgidi wamakhwenkwe: isiso
isiqalekiso
iyamngcungcuthekisa, imthunuka esapholayo isilonda
yomba elavalekayo inxeba
ixhela owaxolayo umxhelo
Kaloku owakhe unyana,
nje ngoThixo, ekuphela komzeleyo
wagqibela ukumbona:
ehamba, ephefumla, engcamla
ethetha, ebona, esiva:
ngala mini emnikezela ezandleni zamadoda

ukuba amenze indoda
naye azohlonitshwa nje ngendoda
atshat'unyanae abenomfazi nabantwana
nje ngamanye amadoda.
Naye lo mama abe ngumhakhulu, ateketise
Le yomgidi imini: Ewayesel'eyilungiselela,
ejong'enkalwen'eyakhel'umkhanyo ngethemba.
Zange imndwendwele. Zange imfikele
Zange walibon'ilanga layo, kuba zange limfikele
Indwendwe alaziyo ngumphanga
Kwimigidi yelali, xa ningamboni eyizimasa lo mama,
maze nincede ningamboni nje ngomntu onomona,
ze nazi ukuba yena ngumzili mhla ngemini zemigidi
Umzili kumzi kaXhosa, akanto kwizici neziyunguma
zelali!
Maze nazi ukuba lo mama ngumzili ongaphezi
oku koMlingi ongaphezi.

A MOURNER WHO DOES NOT STOP
Siwaphiwe Fortune Shweni

It's a big day for families whose boys went to the
mountain
It's an exciting day for meat eaters
It's an exciting day for friends of Dl'omdlayo
It's an exciting day for friends of Mabil'ebanda
It's an exciting day for those who come from the mountain
It's an exciting day for dogs and even pigs as they will also
get the scraps
It's exciting people ululating
people are singing and dancing
people are celebrating with families that sent their sons to
the mountain
and the boys that are coming back from the mountain
There is a parent who is a mother that one day
after handing over her son to the men
So they can make him a man of his home
She opened the door with an unwashed face
wrapped with a white blanket with red lines
To this woman this day of celebration of the boys is a
curse
it tortures her and opens up a wound that healed
it digs a wound that closed
it cuts a soul that was in peace
Her son
was her only child
the last time she saw him
he was walking, breathing, drinking
he was talking, seeing, hearing
that day she handed him over to the men

so they make him a man
so that he will be respected like a man
get married and have a wife and children
Like other men
This woman is to be also a grandmother
This day of celebration that she was preparing for
Preparing for this day with great hope
The day never arrived for her
She never saw that as it never came
The visitor she knows is death
When you see this woman not celebrating with the village
Please do not assume that she is a jealous person
Know that she becomes a mourner on the day of celebration
A mourner in the Xhosa nation does not attend celebrations
Know that this woman is a mourner that does not stop
Like a curse that never ends

Translated from the Xhosa original – Umzili Ongaphezi – *by Innocentia Mhlabi*

ISIKHALO SAMANINA
Yonela Thengimfene
(Xhosa)

Yhoooo! khanindiboleken'iindlebe mzoNtsundu
Khanindiboleken'iindlebe ndigabh'okusembilinini kum
Kub'ub'umzoNtsund'unxunguphele
Umhla nezolo kubulaw'amabhinqa
Kubulaw'amabhinqa kuxhwilw'iintsana
Izigwinta zidal'isankxwe
Namhl'amakhay' angxwelerhekile
Namhl'amakhaya kuzindonga kub'oonozal' itshoba
lilel'umbethe
Kuhuhuz' izihuhulu kunqanqaz'oonogqaza
kutabhat'oonotoyi
Yini! madod'angenalusini
Zadandathek'iintsana zilahl'ithemba
Kub'unozala sisikhukukaz'esifuk'amantshontsho waso
Namhl'iintsana zilala ziqamele ngeenyembezi
Ndihlab'ikhwelo kuni mzoNtsundu!
Kaloku madod'indod' idalelwe ukubangukhuseli
kwibhinqa
Intiyo, inzondo azingesenzelinto
Kaloku sisi sizw'esikhusan'amagxa nesikhothan'amanxeba
Makubeluxolo kubhabh'ubumnyama kuvel'ukukhanya
Makubechosi kubehele!
Nzothololo!!

THE CRY OF WOMEN
Yonela Thengimfene

Yhoo! Lend me your ears Africans
Lend me your ears so I can get this weight off my chest
For the house of Africans is in tatters
Every day women are killed
Women are killed children are being kidnapped
Thugs are causing chaos
Homes are in sorrows
Today homes are hallow and parents do not know what to do
It has become a state of anarchy
Why! Men with no conscience
Children have faded and have lost all hope
Because a mother is the hen that protects its chicks
Today children they sleep in tears
I blow the horn to you Africans
Because men were made to protect women
Hatred will not resolve anything
We are a nation that protects each other and tends to our wounds
Let there be peace, darkness must make way for the light
Let there be peace
Nzothololo!!

Translated from the Xhosa original – Isikhalo Samanina – *by Innocentia Mhlambi*

IZIHANGE
Anelisa Thengimfene
(Xhosa)

Ho! hayi, hayi, hayi!
Ndidlikidlwa luhlanga lwenimba ngaphakathi;
Xa ndibon' mthinjan' uphela zizigwinta!
Zwe lomthonyama limaxongo.
Zwe lomthonyama liyanxakama.
Umhla nezolw' amanin' ayabhomboloza!
Angoomabon' abulawe kwizihange.
Liya phi n' eli lizwe mz' oNtsundu?
Kwaba ngasa kwaphalal' igaz' ezitalatweni!
Sihleli nje sibamb' amazinyo singcwathile!
Kub' asikwazi kuzilwela kwezi zixhiphothi.

Lwaya phi n' uvelwanw' ebantwini?
Bafa becel' uxolw' abasetyhini bengonanga.
Imini nobusuku bazingelw' okwezilwanyana zasendle;
Zizidla mlilw' ezingenalusini.
Kwaba ngas' iimazi zoobawo zincancwa ziimfene!

Kwasa sathukana!
Kwasa sabulalana!
Yeyani na le ndyikityha?
Kwilizwe lonk' alitshoni lingenandaba.
Kubulalan' abamelwane.
Kutyikityan' oogazi linye.
Kwasa kwahlaselw' ibhinqa!
Kwasa kwadlwengulw' ibhinqa!
Khanibeke phants' izikhali mz' oNtsundu;
Khe sithethathethane mawethu.
Singabantwana begazi.

Singabantwana bomthonyama.
Masilwe lo msing' uhlal' uguguma.
Sihleli nje siphil' ubomi bentshontsho,
Lona lilindel' ukuxhwilwa ngukhetshe nanini na!
Siphil' intlalw' entlakantlaka!
Aphi n' amanen' adlan' iindleb' achile lo mshologu?
Agqugule axubushe le ntsindabadala.
Nde-e xhaxhe! Larhosh' irhamba!

SAVAGES
Anelisa Thengimfene

Ho! No, no, no!
I am conflicted with sorrow inside
When I see women vanishing because of thugs!
The nation is in a dire situation
The nation is crying
Women cry and complain every day
They are being killed
Where is this nation headed, Africans?
At dawn blood is spilt
We sit nervously!
For we cannot defend ourselves from these thugs.

What happened to empathy in people?
Women die asking for forgiveness
Day and night they are hunted like wild animals
Animals with no conscience
When it dawns a woman lays dead.

At dawn we swear at one another
At dawn we kill each other
What is this mess about?
A day does not end with no news in the nation
Neighbours are killing each other
Relatives are at one another's throats
At dawn a woman will be attacked
At dawn a woman is raped!
Put your weapons down, Africans
And let's talk to each other

We are siblings
We are children of the soil
Let us fight this wave that always comes back

Translated from the Xhosa original – Izihange *– by Innocentia Mhlambi*

NTWA YA BANA BA THARI
Thabang Tsolo
(Sesotho)

Re phela lefatsheng lena le buswang ke marena, Matona le
moporesidente
Empa marena ha a sa mamelwa
A nyemotswa ka mahlo feela
Hoba polotiki e ba hlwele hodimo,

Bulang mahlo le bone
Lefatshe la bo ntate moholo oa rona, le se le tshwehla
Polotiki e le sentse le ya nyonyeha
Batho ba se ba kwenyana sa diphoofolo tsa naha,

Diroki ho kgale re lwana ntwa ya leleme
Ra hoeletsa mantswe a ba a tjha
Empa batho ba bang bona ba lwana ntwa ya matsoho
Ba kakatletse dibetsa
Ba re bona ha ba batle tharollo ba tlile ntweng
Mmuso ba tla o nka ka mahahapa,

Bonang dipolayano tse Natala
Tse bakuweng ke polotiki
Ditulo di tsekwa ka dithunya
Hoba e se e le moetlo wa bo ra-dipolotiki
Ba rinya monna le mosadi ha ba tsotelle,

Hona jwale bana ba Rantsho ba fedile
Ba qetuwe ke polotiki
Ha e sa le e qala kgale-kgale
Ka dilemo tsa kgethollo ya mmala
Le ha jwale e sa butse mmetso
Batho e ba kwenya bokwiditana.

CIVIL WAR
Thabang Tsolo

We live in a land governed by kings, headmen and a president
But kings are no longer listened to
They are ignored
Because politics have taken over

Open your eyes and see
The land of our forefathers is still boiling
Politics have eroded your values it's disgusting
People now sallow each other like wild animals

Poets have long been fighting for language
Shouting until our voices burnt
Some people are engaged in a fist fight
Carrying weapons
They say they don't want solutions they came to fight
They will take government by force

Behold, massacres in Natal
Caused by politics
Positions are challenged with guns
To politicians it's now a culture
They eliminate both men and women without remorse

There are no more children of the soil left
Consumed by politics
Since it started long ago
During apartheid
Even today it's the same
It swallows them without remorse

Translated from the Sesotho original – Ntwa Ya Bana Ba Thari
– *by Goodenough Mashego*

SELLO SA MMOKOTSANE
Thabang Tsolo
(Setswana)

Utlwang
Lefatshe le ya duma-duma
Le ya dumaela
Ho utlwahala diboko tsa basadi le barwetsana,

Ba kgitla sa masetla-pelo seboko
Ebile monongwaha se kgitlwa le ke ba mantswe a ma tenya
Sello ke sa mmokotsane tlhoriso
Se tsoha basading
Ba re matlung a bona ha hona kgotso
Mmileng moo ba tsamayang teng ha ba bolokeha,

Lefu la matsoho le dula le ba setse morao
Bosiu le motshehare ho ya itshwanela,
Ka mehla le tobane le hlooho tsa bona
Hoba ba phaka di tshetshane ha ba kgone ho itwanela,

Ba lwana ka leleme
Ba re ntwa ke ya madula-mmoho
Athe ba ra-dikotswana ba bang ba kgantsha diphaka le dibetsa
Ho hlola ntwa ha bona ke ho ba fenetha
Batho ba fanyehwa sa diphoofolo
Mohlolo! Ba fenethwa ke batho ba lokelang ho ba tshireletsa
Ha e le ba bang , ba be ba ba thetsitse ka tsa marato
Athe ba batla ho ba kgaolela ditshiu tsa ho phela,

Ka hobane wa bona mohoo o ntse o so utlwahale

Le sello sa bona ha se hlomole dipelo tsa babolai
Le ha jwale basadi ba sa howa ka mantswe a phefa
Ba kopa mmuso o ba sekehele tsebe
O be o phethe toka ho ba bolai.

A WEEPING
Thabang Tsolo

Listen
The world is sending loud echoes
It is roaring
What we hear are the cries of women and daughters,

They blurt a heart-wrenching cry
This year even thick voices are crying
It's a weeping against violence
Started by women
They say there is no peace in their homes
They are not safe on the roads where they walk,

Death trails them
Day or night makes no difference,
They face the same threat every day
Since they are weak they can't fight for themselves,

They fight through their tongues
They say it's domestic violence
Some men flaunt their power and weapons
To win the war for them is to kill them
People are attacked like animals
Surprise! They are killed by people who should protect them
Others were lied to that it was love,
While they want to reduce their days,

Since their crying is still not heard

Their cry also does not find pity in the hearts of their killers

Even today when women cry in low breathing voices
Begging the government to listen to them
And mete justice on their killers.

Translated from the Setswana original – Sello Mmokotsane – *by Goodenough Mashego*

BIRDSONG OF THE EASTERN CAPE
David Jude van Schoor

1
You left it too late to leave here,
Then abandon yourself to song.
Prepare for winter's executions
In cold, unmoving arms.

Condense, a million words,
To love's trochaic refrain:
Two summer syllables,
The spiral of her name.

I was a drinker where the Cape
Honeysuckle clambered,
I was a sunbird weaving
Twigs and strands to a shape.

Now at my lathe I must shift
For I am cutting my cares free,
And confiding my smoother gifts
In the clefts of a pale, bare tree:

For Love and Winter snag
And keep and simplify me.
I am made whole, I am unreft
By a lover's readiness for death.

Condense, my million words,
To love's trochaic refrain:
Two summer syllables,

The spiral of her name.

2

I'll unweave a simpler birdsong
On the needle of her name,
And unthread again my longing
From this tenuous frame.
I stitch this delicate warp
Against her finer weft
I sang three summer's songs
And this is what I left.

Yellowwood love, I have left it
Late to fly, too late to fly you:
Then with this sift of rawer silk,
I pan the rills of winter light
For yellow dust to deck you.

3

While Winter draws her naked
Blades, I scrape the whetstone
Of winter air, the wheel of her refrain:
I am finishing the spinning syllables
Of her fatal, sparking name.

Now my million words are folded,
The knife of love perfected, honed:
I wrap me in a cloth I threaded with song,
And prepare for winter's executions

In her cold and moving arms.

4
She wreathes her limbs
In lunar bracelets
While I loop haphazard songs,
And I wind on long, bare
Fingers, these rugged hoops
of gold and bronze.

Deep in an eastern valley
Lost to the foregone town,
Obscurely we swayed
To our mingled sound,
In cold, unmoving arms.

MATCHBOX
Justin Lyndon Williams

I live in a house close to the tracks. I live in a house –
a matchbox – that shakes when trains roll by.
I live in a house with cracks
in the wall by the kitchen window. I live
in a house that tells you all your neighbours' secrets.
I live in a house where an uninvited wasp flies in every
day with the one o' clock sun. I live in a house that laughs at the wasp
every time she flies thinks she's found freedom and flies
into the window. I live in a house I live in a house that tries
to bake me in the summer. I live in a house that swells her
doors with tears so I can't leave in the winter.

THESE DAYS
Lucas Delisiwe Zulu

These days are strange and spine-chilling and sighing for courage
to bear up the terrible ordeal this year is going through,
its piercing winter amazes me and its gaze an unspoken question.
Its sunlight hours are merely seconds on the main streets,
These long weekends have their little foibles just like the public
Holidays they pass unnoticed and seem to have lost the good times.
these lovely mornings are ink and paper they spill out my thoughts.
these brown eyes are slowly shifting from these turbulent times, drifting to the near future that will never, ever be my past,
a bygone era has vanished into thin air, these cold days an eerie
leap year, dropping bombshells and fabulous things ahead of us,
its coughing months on the road to recovery. When these bleak days
disappear will they come back to haunt us again…

BIOGRAPHIES

Thamsanqa Mlungisi Cindi, also known as The Bard Intellect, was born in Pongola (KZN) on 31 July 1991, out of wedlock. Thamsanqa was fairly raised by both parents and grew up in various parts of the country, but currently residing in Tembisa (Gauteng) with the mother and two siblings. Thamsanqa is an ex-convict who fell in love with writing while behind bars; a teachable spirit who is self-taught and seeking to inspire change.

Born in Cape Town at the turn of the century, **Connor Cogill** is a student and queer writer of colour. He is currently registered for a Bachelor of Arts degree in Language and Culture at Stellenbosch University, engaging his love for philosophy, writing and literature. His works can be found in *New Contrast*, *The Johannesburg Review of Books*, and the upcoming edition of *The Jack Journal*, while he himself can usually be found watching reality TV in his bedroom.

Christine Coates, a poet from Cape Town, holds an MA in Creative Writing from the University of Cape Town. She has three collections of poetry: *Homegrown* (Modjaji Books, 2014), *Fire Drought Water* (Damselfly Press, 2018), and *The Summer We Didn't Die* (Modjaji Books, 2020). Her debut collection Homegrown received an honourable mention from the Glenna Luschei Prize. Her poems and fiction have been published in many local and international literary journals and have been widely anthologised.

Florence Diana de Vries is an English and Afrikaans journalist, essayist and poet who was born in Paarl, South Africa. She writes avidly and regularly traverses themes like loss, memory and travel with insatiable curiosity. She holds a Master of Philosophy (2007) and Bachelor of Philosophy (2004) from Stellenbosch University in Journalism and a Bachelor of Arts (2003) from the University of Cape Town. She has been a corporate communications and brand manager at Stellenbosch University since 2017.

Kimberly Elana Fray is mother of two and married to musician and music tutor Jared Fray. She works as a producer and is also the founder of the Words IN Verse blog. Kimberly was a judge for the South African Writer's Circle in 2020. Her poetry has been published in *New Coin*, *The Kalahari Review* and *Down In The Dirt Magazine*. Some of her latest work has also been accepted in Quillkeepers Press, which is set for release later this year.

Kgalalelo Lebogang Gaebee (née Morwe) is a creative, an avid reader, a social activist, and a blogger. She enjoys writing poems, short stories, and reflections on the present, memories of the past and predictions for the future. She considers her family to be most important to her. If she isn't spending time with them, you can almost always find her taking long walks around her neighbourhood. 'Mosadi gare ga Basadi' is her second poem to be featured in an anthology.

Mamodiehi Gwala is a writer, guitarist, researcher and programme evaluator. She started writing at the tender age of twelve. Poetry became a tool for voicing her feelings and views on a number of personal issues and social ills. Her performance style is a fusion of words and melodies which emanates from her love for jazz and RnB soul. She hopes to help others find comfort and healing through poetry, which she deems a powerful therapeutic tool.

Bhekumuzi Christopher Kubheka, born and raised in KwaZulu-Natal, Durban, is a poetry writer and has self published two poetry books called poetry movement and poetry movement volume II. His love of poetry began from a very young age. He is a member of the playhouse company based in Durban that hosts poetry shows every month end.

Thabiso Tsietsi Lakajoe is a writer of Sesotho poetry and short stories. Lakajoe fights for the rights of the mother tongue so that it can be held and respected like any other South African language. Some of his poems have been published in *Poetry Potion*, *Botsotso*, *BKO*, *Cultural Review*, AvBob Poetry Competition 2019, and the *Sol Plaatje European Union Poetry Anthology* (2015, 2016, 2017 & 2018).

Alinaswe Lusengo is currently a twenty-year-old media and politics student at the University of Cape Town. She is based in both Cape Town and Johannesburg. She is a writer, poet and activist who is interested in all the ways that politics touches even the smallest aspects of our lives. She is an intersectional feminist who dreams of a world where all bodies are safe, comfortable and free.

Tshindane Livhuwani was born in 1969 at Siloam village. She is the last-born daughter of the late Sarah Muofhe Tshindane and Lucas Makhaya Tshindane. She has four children, three sons and one daughter, Ndivhuwo, Fhatuwani, Mikovhe and Munei. She is a teacher by profession and has taught for 16 years at Matanda Primary School in Limpopo (Nzhelele). Her zeal for writing was emulated from her brother the late RP Tshindane who wrote the book Mutambo wa muhumbulo.

Zama Madinana is a Johannesburg-based performer, poet and writer. His work has appeared in *Stanzas*, *Botsotso*, *Carapace*, *Poetry Potion*, *The Thinker*, *Sunday World*, *New Coin* and other literary publications. His work focuses mainly on love, politics and social issues. In 2018, he was longlisted for Sol Plaatje European Union Poetry Award. He holds a Bachelor of Accounting Sciences in Management Accounting and is now pursuing a degree in Creative Writing at the University of South Africa.

Landisile Magwaxaza, born in the former homeland of Transkei, Lady Frere at Mbinzana Village, started school at Holi Lower Primary School, then moved to Mbinzana Higher Primary School where he did standard three and four. Then he moved to Mfanta Junior Secondary School. From Mfanta, he went to Hala Senior Secondary School where he obtained his matric in 1994. He went to Cape Town for greener pastures, and then started writing poetry.

James Mahlangu was born in Moruleng, North West Province. He developed the passion for poetry writing at a young age which helped him express his emotions. He believes in the power that words have to assist us in tackling emotional issues and the comfort they bring. He enjoys listening to music and travelling, seeing new faces and observing different cultures. Nolwazi Mbali Mahlangu is a poet with a theatre and performance certificate from the Duma Ndlovu Actor's Academy and currently part of the Current State of Poetry class of 2020/21. She is the Polokwane Slam Emporium Goddess of the Mic 2018 winner, Ekurhuleni Slam 2018/19 semi-finalist. Her work has been featured on *Confessions*, a Mandla Mpanjukelwa play. She has showcased on 100 Poets for Mandela, 7th Annual Polokwane Literary Fair and the Human Rights Festival at Constitution Hill.

Tshepiso Makgoloane is a diligent writer currently staying in Motetema. She is not just a bookworm with an intense interest in literature and African languages but also a law student. This passionate poet self-published her African award-winning poetry collection book titled *Tša maAfrika with ViaAfrika*, through the WritePublishRead self-publishing programme. The world is eagerly awaiting her other Sepedi poetry collection which is in publication process by the NLSA, Community Publishing Grant. Some of her work has been published in the *Sol Plaatje European Union Poetry Anthology VIII* and on the Avbob poetry project, 2020. This outspoken poet is an eloquent motivational speaker in possession of an achievement certificate in excellent communication and narration and also a certificate of completion in the WPR self-publishing programme.

Charles Julie Makofane was born in 1997 in the village of Leboeng GaMoraba, Limpopo. He is the second child in the family to study BALP at the University of Venda. In 2015, at the age of eighteen, he began writing, without publishing until 2020.

Tebogo Patricia Mamabolo is a writer, poet and

published author of a poetry book called *Ge ke Ithekola*. Tebogo holds a chemistry qualification and postgraduate diploma in business management. Tebogo received first prize in the 2019 Avbob Poetry Competition in the Sepedi category, her winning poem 'Palo ya dikgare' is published in the *I Wish I'd Said Vol.3* anthology. In her free time, Tebogo likes to read and write to empower herself to a greater level.

Maakomele R Manaka is a Soweto-born poet with a master's degree in creative writing, four collections of poetry: *If Only* (2003), *In Time* (Geko, 2009) *Flowers of a Broken Smile* (InkSword, 2016) and *Oncoming Traffic* (Botsotso, 2018) and a dub-poetry album Word Sound Power (MelodyMuzik, 2008). Manaka's poetry has appeared in various literary journals locally and internationally, translated to German and Italian. He has been invited to literary festivals around the globe. Manaka performed his poetry for both former presidents, Mr Thabo Mbeki and the late Mr Nelson Mandela.

Adré Marshall has taught English at various universities including UCT, where she was awarded a PhD. Her poetry has been published in numerous journals, including *Carapace*, *New Contrast*, *English Academy Review* and *Stanzas*, and the anthologies *Absolute Africa!*, *Earth Africa!*, and *Coming Home: Poems of the Grahamstown Diaspora*. She has appeared as a guest poet at the McGregor Poetry Festival and other events and is the author of a book on Henry James.

Keketso Adorn Mashigo is the author of a shortstory collection entitled *SOFINA is Not the End*, a poet and co-author of an essay anthology entitled *Shadows of Their*

Mothers and a book reviewer at *Pulp Review*. He is also a proofreader and freelance journalist. His work has appeared in many different publications including *Loocha* magazine, *New Coin*, *Pangolin Review*, *Praxis Online* and *Avbob Poetry*. Keketso lives in Madjembeni, Mpumalanaga.

Zongezile Matshoba works at the South African Museum of Literature in Makhanda. You will find him in your township or village or school or town or hall or open ground, and wherever there is a literature-related event for the young and old. His writings narrate the humour and hardships of township and rural life, and interrogate whether it is yet uhuru in people's livelihood.

Mzoli Mavimbela is the first born of four siblings, two boys and one girl, from Nyawuza clan. He was born to Zolani Mavimbela and Nodumo Bangani of the Khiwa clan. Mzoli grew up in the beautiful landscapes and mountainous areas of Port St Johns, Eastern Cape. He attended Zanokhanyo High School Gcinumthetho. He is a qualified social worker at SANCA in George, Western Cape Province. He is currently doing a Master's degree in Social Work (Research) at Nelson Mandela University and he aims to do PhD later. To date he has written five books: *Chosi Chosi Ntsomi* (Mbana Designs & Printing, 2016), *Zigqitywa Kuhlwile Zibonwe Liwuhlabile* (Centre for the Book, 2020–2021), *Zezani Na Ezi Zililo?* (Mbana Designs & Printing, 2019), *Masibuyel' Embo Konakele Phi Na?* (Weza Home Publishing, 2021), *Siqhaqh' Amabholo* (Kotaz Magazine Publishers, forthcoming). Hi poems have appeared in www.avbobpoetry.co.za, *AMAZWI Trilingual Poetry Magazine*, *Complexities, transitions and developmental challenges: the case of the Eastern Cape Province* (forthcoming) and the *Sol Plaatje European Poetry*

Anthology. In 2019 he won a best national author award at APAPA (African Print Authors & Poetry Awards).

Based in Johannesburg, **Frank Meintjies** has worked in the field of social development. Frank's creative writing has been included in several South African anthologies. He also frequently contributes to the world of poetry through participation in readings. Frank's poetry collections are *Unfettered Days* (2015), *Connexions* (2012) and *My Rainbow* (2009). He also has written several children's stories and short stories.

Mandlakayise Mfanta was born in 1976 in Cofimvaba in the Eastern Cape. He has a diploma in security management from Unisa. His interest in writing developed while he was young. He has just finished writing a Xhosa novel and is also currently busy writing another one whilst looking for a publisher. He collaborated with two friends to write and self publish a book, *Isithebe* (Xhosa poems).

Mmabore Gladys Mogashoa was born at GaMogashoa village in Sekhukhune area, Limpopo. She is the 2019 Provincial Innovation Award winner for Golden Shield Heritage Awards and May Essay competition winner titled 'I am an African' from National Heritage Council of South Africa. She was awarded Best Newcomer for Skeem Local Music Awards and a heritage activist for the Benchmarks Foundation. Her 2020 Sepedi music ulbum is titled *Gasekhukhune*. Her song 'Climate Change' won third place in the 2020 Just Recovery Art Challenge.

Siza Nkosi Mokhele is a published author and poet with an MA in Creative Writing from Rhodes University and a PhD candidate. She is presently a creative writing lecturer at the Sol Plaatje University and CEO of the House of Siza, an NPO that seeks to change people's lives through music, literature and art. Her poetry is featured in local and international literary journals and anthologies. She published nine children's story books with Oxford University Press. In 2020 she curated Reflection Session on June 16, 1976, Credo Mutwa Intergenerational Colloquium and 57th Commemoration of Miriam Makeba's UN Speech.

Nedine Moonsamy is a senior lecturer in the English department at the University of Pretoria. She is currently writing a monograph on contemporary South African fiction and otherwise conducts research on science fiction in Africa. Her debut novel, *The Unfamous Five* (Modjaji Books) was shortlisted for the HSS Fiction Award (2021), and her poetry was previously awarded third place in the Sol Plaatje European Union Award (2013) and shortlisted for the inaugural New Contrast National Poetry Award (2021).

Mapule Ramaila Moswane was born in Thabampje village, Ga-Masemola Makhuduthamaga District Municipality, Limpopo. She attended Thabampje Primary School and Matlebjoane Secondary School in the same village. After obtaining her undergraduate degree, and a diploma, she worked as a teacher at Maphadime, Mampuru-Tseke, and Matlebjoane Secondary schools respectively. She then moved to Cape Town where she works as a language practitioner at the Parliament of RSA. She is passionate about creative writing, in particular poetry.

Aphiwe Namba, originally from Durban, started writing and directing his own plays after training at DUT in a three-year national diploma in drama and production studies, from 2011 to 2013. He received a cameo award in 2011, a best actor award in 2012 for Creon in *Antigone*, and also won a creative achievement award for musical direction in *Nawe Mbopha kaSithayi* in which he played the lead role of Mbopha kaSithayi. In 2013 he received another creative achievement award for musical direction in *Untombazi*. His plays include: *Halfway House* (City Lights Film Script), *Us Against Them*, *Amongst Men*, *Confessions* and *Babazile*.

Kwazi Ndlangisa is a multi-award-winning poet from South Africa, published writer and translator based in UMzimkhulu, KZN. His writings are a golden thread through Africanism and spirituality, and are inspired by his surroundings as well as his inner being. He believes that writing and reading poetry is a perfect channel to bring the self to its true purpose, in both the psychological and spiritual realm. Ndlangisa is the author of *Collecting Self* and has been published in poetry anthologies and in online magazines, namely the *Sol Plaatje European Union Poetry Anthology* (SA), *Yesterdays and Imagined Realities: An Anthology of South African Poetry* (SA/France), *Reflections from the Margins, Complexities, transitions and developmental challenges: the case of the Eastern Cape Province, Di-vêrsé-city Annual Anthology* (USA), *The Grayots of Ubuntu: An Anthology of Contemporary Poetry from Africa* (Kenya), and *Gcwala Creative Writing Magazine* (SA).

Mawushe Selby Nomnganga is a community development worker using the popular education methodology. Nomnganga also does freelance reporting mainly with *Groundup*, an online publication. At the moment Nomnganga is the project coordinator of AOPESH (Advice Office 4 Personal, Environmental Safety and Health), an advice office aiming to develop systems and organisational forms that are resilient in responding to COVID-19 induced changes.

Azile Ntloni is a twenty-one-year-old from Flagstaff in the Eastern Cape province, but currently stays in Durban. Ntloni is a part-time student, motivated by her love of learning and succeeding as she strives to become an outstanding and successful woman in today's generation. She became a poet at an early age, and she keeps writing poems in the hope of changing people's lives.

Sihle Ntuli is a South African poet living in Durban. His poetry was shortlisted for the DALRO Poetry Prize in 2017. He is the author of the poetry chapbook *Rumblin* (uHlanga Press, 2020). His work has appeared in notable South African and African publications, including the anthology *Years of Fire and Ash: South African Poems of Decolonization* (Jonathan Ball, 2021).

Mosima Kagiso Phakane (b.1996) is a writer from Ga-Matlala Kordon in Limpopo, South Africa. She has won the Avbob poetry contest in the Sepedi category (2017) and her work has been featured in *Ake Review* (2020), *Unisa Press: Education as Change* (2020), *Avbob Poetry I Wish I'd Said* anthologies (2018/2019), *Sol Plaatje European Union Poetry Anthology* (2019), *Poetry Potion* and *Odd* magazine. Mosima is the co-author of Seasonal Aspects of our Lives poetry book.

Yvonne Phyllis works as the co-director of operations at The Forge (https://theforge.org.za), a pan-African radical space in Johannesburg, Braamfontein. Prior to joining The Forge, Yvonne worked as a lecturer at the University Currently Known as Rhodes. She taught comparative politics and international relations in the Department of Political and International Studies. Born to farm workers in one of the most impoverished towns in the Eastern Cape, Bedford, Yvonne's research interests include farm workers/dwellers' lived experiences and struggles, the struggles of black first-generation graduates, equality and land reform and redistribution in South Africa.

Tshifhiwa Itai Ratshiungo is a writer and creative currently studying law at the University of the Free State. His work has been previously published in *AfricanWriter*, *Yesterdays and Imagined Realities: An Anthology of South African Poetry* (Impepho Press), *Archive of Forgetfulness* and elsewhere. He is available online @_tshifhiwa.

Warren Jeremy Rourke is currently the commissioning editor and senior agent for the South Africa-based, internationally engaged, World Arts Agency (WAA). He has been appointed as the managing editor of Africa's newest literary journal, *Hotazel Review* (forthcoming, 2021). His poems have been published in *New Contrast*, his short fiction in *Botsotso*, and his painting in *Sharp!* He is also a spoken word poet, having performed online through DANC (Disabled Artists Networking Community, UK). Rourke lives with BD-1 disability.

Noluthando Mpho Sibisi is a South African storyteller who makes use of writing, performance and visual art as modes of complicating, archiving and canonising South African black women narratives. They hold an honours degree in English literature and drama directing from Rhodes University and are currently completing their Masters in Theatre and Performance at the University of Cape Town.

Born in Bloemfontein, **Dimakatso Anthea Sedite**'s poems have appeared in *Teesta Review*, *Brittle Paper*, *New Coin*, *Kalahari Review*, *BKO*, *Best New African Poets*, *Botsotso*, *Aerodrome*, *Brave Voices*, *Poéfrika*, *Poetry Potion* and *Hello Poetry*, with two more due to appear in *Stanzas*. She is the joint winner of the 2019 DALRO Prize. She holds an MA in research psychology from the University of the Witwatersrand. Her debut poetry collection is forthcoming from Deep South in 2021.

Moses Seletiša is a Sepedi performance poet and author whose area of interest is African languages and its social context. He is the first person to have won a Sol Plaatje European Union Poetry Award in a language other than English and Afrikaans. He was the winner of a South African Literary Award as first-time published author, and awarded a Young Heritage Activist Award, under the National Heritage Council of South Africa. He is from Ga-Matlala 'a Rakgoadi in rural Limpopo, where he lives.

Siwaphiwe Fortune Shweni is an Eastern Cape-born award-winning poet who writes mainly in Xhosa. He is a product of Tshatshatsha Primary School, Freemantle Boys' High School and Cape Peninsula University of Technology. He won third place in the 2019 AVBOB poetry competition and won the prize in 2020. His work is published locally, in print and online.

I am **Yonela Thengimfene**, my navel is in the land of Ngqamakhwe. I am a Xhosa who grew up speaking Xhosa fluently. I have received a basic education from the mother hen that gave birth to me, mother Nomini Thengimfene. There was always a thin hen with thick wings. Today I am proud of my mother tongue. I am inspired by Ngxabane's colleague Dr Yolisa Madolo for his love of the Xhosa language. A long fire shall quench the fire, and they shall be consumed with fire.

Anelisa Thengimfene is a poet and Xhosa indie author. She is originally from Ngqamakhwe, Eastern Cape, South Africa. In 2016 she met Xhosa legend, Dr Yolisa Madolo, who inspired her to write. She has published a number of poems at www.avbobpoetry.co.za, *Amazwi* magazine, National Library of South Africa, *Left Behind: Developmental DILEMMAS of the Eastern Cape province*. She has published two books, *Ithunga Lizala Ngumphehlulu* and *Ithiwani Xa Inje?* She is a BA honour's student at Nelson Mandela University.

Thabang Tsolo is a native of Jouberton, near the town of Klerksdorp. He is a writer/poet who uses Sesotho in all his writing. He started before writing only poems, but now he is involved in other writings such as short stories, stories and more. In 2018 he successfully published his first book on Smashwords, under the auspices of WPR and Via Afrika.

David Jude van Schoor (born in Cape Town, 1977) studied at UCT until 2001, when he went to live in Japan. He has taught and researched at universities in Europe and South Africa. He has degrees in Latin poetry (UCT) and Greek drama (University of Zurich). He is currently senior lecturer in Greek and Latin at Rhodes University. He is working on a novel about the lives of early family in 20th-century District Six and a collection of poems, *Drought Songs*.

Justin Lyndon Williams is from Elsies River, Cape Town. He is currently reading for an English MA in Creative Writing at the University of the Western Cape. He holds a BA Honours degree from UWC. He writes short fiction and poetry on topics ranging from existential crises to social decay. Some of his work has appeared in *WritingThreeSixty* and *New Contrast*.

Lucas Delisiwe Zulu is a poet, writer and anthologist who lives in Emalahleni, Kwa-guqa, Mpumalanga. His poems have appeared in *Diverse Voices: An Anthology of Courage* (Tarifi Press, 2021). He enjoys creative writing.

WHAT IS THE EUROPEAN UNION?

The European Union (EU) is a unique economic and political union between 27 European countries[1] that together cover much of the European continent. The EU was created in the aftermath of World War II. The first steps were to foster economic cooperation: the idea being that countries that trade with one another become economically interdependent and so more likely to avoid conflict.

Since its birth, the union has developed into a single market with the euro (€) as its common currency. What began as a purely economic union has evolved into an organisation spanning policy areas from external relations and security, justice and migration to health, environment and climate. With the global COVID-19 pandemic, Green Recovery has taken centre stage.

The single or 'internal' market is the EU's main economic engine, enabling most goods, services, money and people to move freely. Another key objective is to develop this huge resource also in other areas like energy, knowledge and capital markets to ensure that its citizens can draw the maximum benefit from it.

The EU is based on the rule of law: everything it does is founded on treaties, voluntarily and democratically agreed by its member countries. It actively promotes human rights

---

[1] At the time of writing, Belgium, Bulgaria, Croatia, Czech Republic, Denmark, Germany, Estonia, Ireland, Greece, Spain, France, Italy, Cyprus, Latvia, Lithuania, Luxembourg, Hungary, Malta, the Netherlands, Austria, Poland, Portugal, Romania, Slovenia, Slovakia, Finland and Sweden.

and democracy and in 2012 was awarded the Nobel Peace Prize for advancing the causes of peace, reconciliation, democracy and human rights in Europe.

How does it work?
EU member states have set up institutions to run the EU and adopt its legislation. The main ones are:
- The European Parliament (representing the people of Europe)
- The Council of the European Union (representing national governments)
- The European Commission (representing the common EU interest)

Size and population
The EU is less than half the size of the United States covering some 4 million square kilometres. In terms of size, France is the EU's largest country and Malta its smallest. The EU has a population of close to 450 million people – the world's third largest after China and India.

EU symbols
- The European flag – The 12 stars in a circle symbolise the ideals of unity, solidarity and harmony among the peoples of Europe.
- The European anthem – The melody used to symbolise the EU comes from Ludwig Van Beethoven's 9th Symphony composed in 1823.
- Europe Day – The ideas behind the EU were first put forward on 9 May 1950 by French foreign minister, Robert Schuman. This is why 9 May is celebrated as a key date for the EU.
- The EU motto – "United in diversity".

The EU's economy
Operating as a single market, the EU is a major world trading power. The EU's unique social market economy allows its economies to grow and to reduce poverty and inequality. EU economic policy focuses on creating jobs and boosting growth by making smarter use of financial resources, removing obstacles to investment and providing visibility and technical assistance to investment projects. Small and medium-sized enterprises form the backbone of the EU's economy.

The EU and South Africa – a partnership of equals
Since 1994 the growing relationship between South Africa and the EU has been underpinned by the Trade, Development and Cooperation Agreement (TDCA). Closer ties between the two parties were consolidated in 2007 with the establishment of the EU-SA Strategic Partnership. This partnership, the only one of its kind with an African country, is centred on enhanced political dialogue around issues of shared interest, including climate change, the global economy, governance, bilateral trade, and peace and security matters. In line with this, its action plan encompasses sectoral cooperation on a range of issues such as climate change, environment, education, science and technology, space, trade and migration. Regular high-level meetings steer the partnership, along with the EU-South Africa Joint Cooperation Council. They provide the occasions to discuss current bilateral, regional and global issues.

Trade and investment
The EU is not only South Africa's biggest trading partner but remains its dominant source of Foreign Direct Investment

(40.6%). EU-generated investments have created in excess of 350 000 direct jobs. South Africa's total trade with the EU is in the region of €33 billion. More importantly, 60% of South Africa's exports to the EU consist of agri-food and manufactured goods, which contribute directly to beneficiation and employment and thus to inclusive growth. The entry into force of the SADC-EU Economic Partnership Agreement is generating new opportunities to further strengthen bilateral trade and investment relations.

Development cooperation

The bilateral EU cooperation programme in South Africa provides support to the value of €281 million with additional funding being channelled for thematic focus areas in the form of grants. In addition to that, the total official support of the EU to sustainable development in South Africa includes programmes such as the Erasmus+ programme, and joint EU-South Africa Science and Innovation cooperation through the European Commission's Horizon 2020 Programme. The European Investment Bank makes available some €462 million in long-term loans and there are significant bilateral cooperation programmes between EU Member States and South Africa.